Learn Mandarin Chinese Workbook for Beginners

A Step-by-Step Textbook to Practice the Chinese Characters Quickly and Easily While Having Fun

Leo W. Chang

Learn Mandarin Chinese for Beginners

A Step-by-Step Guide to Master the Chinese Language Quickly and Easily While Having Fun

Leo W. Chang

contained within this document, including, but not limited to, errors, omissions, or inaccuracies.

Table of Contents

Introduction

The decision to pick up another language is not an easy one. Many want to learn Mandarin but look at the traditional style of writing and automatically think it is too difficult. This is where congratulations is necessary, as you took the next step into learning a language that is revolutionizing the world as we know it. No matter what your reasoning is for wanting to learn Mandarin, this book will be with you every step of the way, guiding you through the easiest ways to learn Mandarin in manners that are fun and educational.

Coupled with this book is a workbook that will provide you with hands-on practice for learning to both read and write Mandarin. It will teach you the order of brush strokes, how some Mandarin characters were created, as well as their meaning. But first, one needs to delve into a bit of history, as that is where true interest is cultivated.

Mandarin has been an important language throughout history, from its use as morse code in wars to its role in communicating assassination notices. Mandarin has become ingrained within modern society, with more individuals wanting to learn the language than ever before.

In 2016, a study was done by Global Exam, where they recorded 40 million students learning and preparing for the Hanyu Shuiping Kaoshi (HSK), also written in Mandarin as 汉语水平考试, which is a test that evaluates Mandarin language proficiency. The Global Exam further mentioned that they expect a number of no less than 100 million students learning to prepare for the HSK in 2020, a number that has been exceeded.

Embedded within Mandarin are a bunch of different meanings. What is meant by this is that as you start to learn about the different tones in

Mandarin, especially those related to pinyin, you will begin to understand the intricacies of the language. A different tone given the same character can easily have a completely alternate meaning. That's why this book has been carefully structured in order to ensure that readability is maximized.

With the Mandarin language having many little intricacies that need to be effectively understood, for example, the direction of brush strokes when writing Mandarin characters, it can seem rather difficult when starting off. However, this book is written by those who understand the difficulties of the Mandarin language, as well as the pitfalls that many fall into when learning the language. This is exactly what this book aims to ameliorate.

Although we want you all to learn and be as fluent in Mandarin as you can possibly be, it will not happen overnight. Learning a new language will take lots of time, repetition and dedication. What you put in, is what you will get out. This book intends to act as a resource that creates a strong foundation for learning Mandarin. You may find that as you progress, you start to forget the basics. This is one of the reasons that *Learn Mandarin Chinese for Beginners* was created—to ensure that your basic Mandarin skills are always top-notch.

A memory that reinforced the creation of this book was my own journey in learning Mandarin. The excitement of booking your next HSK test was often coupled with a large number of sleepless nights before the test. The amount of time I had used to focus on the repetition, speech, and characters could probably have earned me a good sum of money.

However, the feeling of passing and receiving your HSK certificate, allowing you to move on to the next level, is such a surreal feeling. You see, Mandarin is more than just memorizing a bunch of characters; it integrates history with current teachings, ensuring that the cultural aspect of the Mandarin language is not mitigated.

You have taken the first step in learning Mandarin. Remember the level of excitement that you are currently feeling. Ensure that you stay motivated and dedicated to your own learning, as it is with self-discipline that you will be conversing in Mandarin with all of your friends. Whether you are learning Mandarin as a party trick, because you find Chinese culture interesting, or you are planning to immigrate to an Asian country that speaks Mandarin, the journey starts now.

Chapter 1:

The History of Mandarin

Understanding the history of Mandarin will allow you to appreciate the development of the language from many different dynasties to the dialect of Mandarin that we utilize today. With Mandarin being the official language of both mainland China, as well as Taiwan, it does not mean that it is not spoken in other countries around the world. Singapore and many other countries of the United Nations recognize Mandarin as one of their official languages. With that being said, it is currently the most widely-spoken language across the world.

As with many languages that are ingrained in history, there is a rather large multitude of dialects that exist. Dialects are not languages per se, and are rather seen as a subset of a language that is spoken in a specific city or country. There are many different versions of Mandarin that are spoken in the various provinces within China. For example, in Hong Kong, Cantonese, a specific dialect of Mandarin, is spoken.

Many times, there are only subtle differences in the different dialects, which can thankfully be identified in their written form since they can be quite confusing for new learners. The reason for this identification is that the standard Mandarin characters are used when communicating in the written form, which heightens the degree to which those conversing understand each other, even though their spoken dialects are mutually unintelligible.

Believe it or not, there are what we call language families and groups. Mandarin is a part of the Chinese family of languages, which is seen as a subsection of the Sino-Tibetan language group. Ever since the beginning of Mandarin's creation, it has been labeled the tonal language, meaning that the manner in which specific characters are pronounced will dictate their meaning. With Mandarin having four tones, some other languages that fall under the Chinese language family have up to ten distinct tones. This means that when we hear the word "Mandarin", we need to tread with caution as it actually has two meanings when used to refer to language.

Mandarin can refer to a specific language group or as its better-known reference, being that of the Beijing dialect of mainland China's standard language. To create some context, the Mandarin language group includes both standard Mandarin (mainland China's official language), and Jin (also referred to as Jin-yu), a language spoken by occupants of inner Mongolia and the central-north region of China.

When referring to *Language Atlas of China*, there is a division whereby eight different dialects are spoken. How these eight divisions differ is via the manner that the Middle Chinese entering tone is utilized. In order to provide some geographical context, we have included the eight divisions below:

- Northeastern Mandarin is spoken by approximately 98 million individuals. Typically, this form of Mandarin is spoken in all places of Manchuria except in the Liaodong Peninsula. Since there is a very strong similarity with standard Chinese, there are very few tonal differences that establish a differentiation.
- Beijing Mandarin is spoken by approximately 27 million individuals. Typically spoken in Beijing along with in Chengde and Northern Hebei, it has begun to branch further into areas such as northern Xinjiang. With the Beijing dialect forming the basis of standard Chinese, one would expect there to be more individuals who speak it. However, it is because many researchers group Beijing Mandarin and Northeastern Mandarin together based on similarity that the number of people who speak these two dialects respectively are combined.
- Jilu Mandarin is localized to the Hebei and Shandong provinces, with approximately 89 million individuals speaking this dialect. There are marked differences regarding the tones

and vocabulary when compared to standard Chinese, leading to zero understanding when conversing with the latter.

- Jiao Liao Mandarin shows a very large degree of variance when compared to Beijing Mandarin. Typically, this variance has resulted in only 35 million individuals speaking the dialect. With very noticeable changes in tone, it is primarily spoken by the Shandong and Liaodong Peninsulas.

- Central Plains Mandarin, spoken by approximately 186 million individuals, is typically found in the central parts of Shaanxi, eastern Gansu, and southern Xinjiang. There is marked intelligibility when compared to Beijing Mandarin, primarily due to the phonological differences.

- Lanyin Mandarin is spoken by 17 million individuals across the central and western Gansu province, as well as in the Ningxia autonomous region.

- Lower Yangtze Mandarin is spoken in Jiangsu and Anhui by approximately 86 million individuals. Typically, there are marked phonological and lexical differences, establishing a sense of intelligibility when compared to Beijing Mandarin.

- A dialect spoken by approximately 260 million individuals is Southwestern Mandarin. Spoken by the Guizhou, Yunnan, Sichuan and Hubei provinces, the sharp tonal, phonological, and lexical changes establish marked intelligibility with Beijing Mandarin.

As history progressed, the term "Mandarin" was initially used by the Portuguese to refer to Imperial Chinese court magistrates when referring to the language that they spoke. However, as Mandarin moved closer toward the Western world, the Chinese themselves starting referring to the language as pǔtōng huà (普通话), guó yǔ (国语), or huá yǔ (華语). Delving deeper into these three variants, pǔ tōng huà directly translates to "common language", referring to the language that is spoken by inhabitants of mainland China. Guó yǔ means "national language" and is used by those in Taiwan, with huá yǔ also having the same meaning, but it is used by those residing in Singapore and Malaysia.

Delving a bit deeper into the history of Mandarin, many have the following question: How did Mandarin actually become China's official language? Given its geographical size, China consists of a wide variety of different languages and dialects. However, it was in the Ming Dynasty (1368 - 1644) that Mandarin emerged as the language of choice by the ruling class.

The Beijing dialect became associated with Mandarin in the latter part of the Ming Dynasty. China's capital changed from Nanjing to Beijing, remaining as Beijing throughout the Ming and Qing Dynasties. With Mandarin being the language of the ruling class, it naturally became the language of choice in courts, as well as amongst the public who were interacting with these courts. Officials from different provinces in China continued to migrate to mainland China, needing to adapt their dialects in order to communicate in court. However, it was not until 1909 that Mandarin became the national language of China.

Typically, when a dynasty falls, there is a change in the main language of the country. However, when the Qing dynasty fell in 1912, Mandarin remained the main language utilized in the Republic of China. To commemorate the fall of the Qing Dynasty, it was renamed as pǔ tōng huà in 1955. Although this renaming was adopted by most of the countries that used Mandarin as an official language, some countries like Taiwan continue to refer to Mandarin as guó yǔ.

Mandarin uses Chinese characters, known as Hànzì (漢字), as its writing system, however, these characters have their own history. Chinese characters appeared over 2,000 years ago, represented as images of real objects. However, as time progressed, the characters became more stylized and started representing ideas as well as objects. With that being said, many characters can comprise two or more ideas, all illustrated differently based on the direction and amount of brush strokes present.

Each Chinese character represents a specific syllable of the Chinese language. However, it needs to be acknowledged that there are many Chinese characters that cannot be used independently as they wouldn't make sense on their own. It is usually the Chinese writing system that deters individuals from wanting to learn Mandarin. However, although it definitely has a certain complexity about it, there are many modern-day tips that can be used to master this writing system.

According to the *Kangxi Dictionary* (康熙字典), there are 47,035 Chinese characters. With there being quite a few historical Chinese character formations that were possibly not registered in the *Kangxi Dictionary*, the actual number to this day remains a mystery. However, do not let this number scare you, as there are really only 3,500 basic Chinese characters that are used for everyday communication. As everything does, Chinese characters have evolved over thousands of years. Their scripts and styles have been changed to form what we now know as freehand cursive, or Xing Shu (行書).

Oracle bone inscriptions were the first depictions of Chinese characters, and they were typically seen as inscriptions on the carapaces of mammals and tortoises during the Shang Dynasty (1600 - 1046 BCE). These inscriptions were typically used for divination, leading it to being called "bu ci" (卜辭).

With there being approximately 4,000 different inscriptions recorded in history, only a thousand of them have successfully been deciphered. As the Shang Dynasty led into the Zhou Dynasty (1046 - 256 BCE), bronze inscriptions were noticed on ritual wine vessels and other bronze objects. There were a further 4,000 different bronze inscriptions present, with more than half of them being successfully understood today.

As the Zhou Dynasty led into the Qin Dynasty (221 - 207 BCE), small seal characters gained popularity. It is here that various scripts began to be adopted by different parts of the Chinese empire. It is also here where, along with the country's unification, the Qin Dynasty's first emperor simplified and unified the written Chinese language. Many of the characters that were seen during this period had a large influence on the standardization of the current Chinese characters.

Official script was then developed during the Han Dynasty (206 BCE - 220 CE). The integration of brush strokes and curves in character writing gained momentum during this time period, symbolizing the shift of Chinese characters into the characters that we make use of today.

Regular script was developed as a by-product of official script, becoming apparent in the southern and northern dynasties (420 - 589 CE). Stylistically, there were alterations made, opening the doors to the artform known today as calligraphy. It is from this point that the mainstream script was developed, with there being no major alterations occurring. Cursive writing appeared right after regular script, with individuals finding a more rapid way to draw Chinese characters. The disadvantage of this form of writing is that if one is not trained in reading combined strokes, there is little to no chance that the total meaning will be able to be fully understood.

China started to realize that the characters used started to become too complicated, leading to a drastic drop in literacy levels in the 1950s. It was during this time that the Chinese government decided to introduce simplified characters to aid in the learning and understanding of the Chinese writing system. What many forget is that there are thousands of characters that need to be practiced and memorized if one wants to master the written language. However, although a simplified character system was adopted by mainland China, Malaysia, and Singapore, Taiwan and Hong Kong have chosen to continue with the use of the traditional characters.

Wanting to provide those who are not native to China with the opportunity to learn the language, romanization was introduced. Students have the ability to utilize the Western alphabet to represent the sounds that are spoken in Mandarin. For those just starting out, this is the typical first step, as it allows there to be a bridge between the studying of Chinese characters and learning the spoken language.

The system that is adopted with teaching materials is Pinyin. With Pinyin superseding older romanization systems, especially zhuyin, it was adopted as the standard method of romanization in 1982. This set off a wide rally of acceptance as the United Nations followed suite in 1986. Singapore, the Library of Congress of the United States, as well as the American Library Association, have adopted pinyin as the most modern method of romanization.

When referring to the spelling of Chinese geographical and personal names, pinyin has made the process that much easier. Pinyin has established a bridging whereby translation from Mandarin to English is easier than before, further being utilized as one of the main methods by which Mandarin is being input into computers. The learning of pinyin has become mandatory across all Mandarin-speaking countries. Where there is more than one language being spoken as an official language, as is the case in Taiwan, irrespective of which language the child grows up learning, he/she will be taught Mandarin in elementary school.

The development of pinyin has increased the rate at which non-Chinese individuals are able to learn Mandarin. Pinyin has made it that much easier to self-study the language, allowing formerly illiterate individuals a better chance at integrating themselves into areas where Mandarin is the main language that's spoken.

Coupled with Chinese characters, pinyin has enabled many foreigners to learn the pronunciation of Mandarin whilst also explaining both the grammatical and spoken domains of the language. However, when we look into the pinyin usage in Taiwan, a country that purely uses traditional Chinese characters, a modified pinyin system called Tongyong Pinyin was created. Today, when visiting Taiwan, one will see the spelling of roads and stores in Tongyong Pinyin.

Although many, especially those from the older generations, were against the adoption of Tongyong Pinyin, the Taiwanese government created a system where legally, a Taiwanese citizen can choose which form of romanization they want on their legal documents. For example, when applying for a new passport, the personal names could be written in Wade-Giles, Tongyong, or Hoklo of Hakka.

Chapter 2:

Where Can Mandarin Be Used?

Mandarin has been growing in popularity, with five countries listing it as an official language. These countries all have more than 50% of their population speaking Mandarin, clocking in at approximately 1.3 billion individuals speaking the language worldwide. The countries that make up this number are China, Taiwan, Hong Kong, Singapore, and Macao. With that being said, there are 19 other countries where Mandarin hasbeen adopted, though this is to a lesser extent.

A lot of people find that learning Mandarin opens many doors for them, especially in terms of career options. Translators and even educators are very popular jobs, especially in countries where Mandarin is an official language. The reason these jobs are well sought after is primarily due to the language barrier that prevents residents of Mandarin-speaking countries from interacting with other countries where Mandarin is not an official language.

Not only does this promote greater communication and development across various countries, but it allows for heightened degrees of innovation as Chinese individuals will now be able to participate on global platforms without fearing that having learned Mandarin will be to their detriment. Contrary to that, learning Mandarin further increases the degree of innovation a person or company experiences as the pool of applicants from which one can choose rises dramatically.

Education opportunities increase even more once one invests the time and effort into learning Mandarin. These opportunities cover both in-school and external schooling, where an exchange becomes possible. Many students, especially in the United States of America, do a school exchange where they visit China and participate in intensive language classes in an attempt to get into a better education system.

With China near the top of the worldwide rankings in terms of their quality of education, finding an avenue to enter into their schooling system should not be disregarded. There is an increasingly popular trend that international students are following that is choosing China as an area to continue studies.

China is the fourth most popular destination for travel, having the third-largest population of international students. This number falls very closely behind those of the US and UK. However, the trend that has been noticed the most is an increase in 10% per year across the past decade, making China one of the most popular study-abroad destinations in the world. When we compare this data to that of ten years ago, when a third of all China's international students were from South Korea, the level of diversity that is currently present is astronomical.

South Korea's contribution to the international student populace in China has dropped to 17%, primarily due to the options and reputations of Chinese universities now reaching further across the world. As of 2019, there were more than 20,000 students present across 13 cities in China, while in the past, most of the students were studying in Beijing or Shanghai. Other popular cities where international students prefer to study include Guangdong in the south of China and Liaoning in the northern area of Beijing.

Previously, there used to be a very large monetary implication for students who have wanted to study in China. However, China focuses on recruiting the most talented, providing them with state-of-the-art equipment and teaching facilities in order for them to really make a difference. The Chinese government has therefore invested heavily in establishing a financial support model that attracts international students. With more than 277 institutions providing over 40,000 scholarships, it should not come as a surprise that international students are flocking toward the opportunities that China is offering.

In 2015, approximately 40% of all international students were on a scholarship that was offered by the Chinese government. When we compare this data to that of 2006, there has been more than a 5-fold increase in the amount of scholarships offered. Typically, the government will provide both language classes and education in order to ensure that the international student is well equipped for learning and is effectively able to positively contribute to society.

Mandarin is further used in many streams of entertainment, which are starting to be readily adopted internationally. Given the current worldwide climate, there has been an increased uptake in not only listening to music that is in another language, but also watching television shows that provide subtitles. The globalization of the Chinese entertainment network has only proven to be of benefit to the populace as it has created an alternative revenue stream for the country.

Along with Mandarin, other languages that have started to become globalized include Japanese and Korean. For each of these three languages, there is a specific theme that has resulted in their worldwide adoption. For Korea, it was the introduction and uptake of Korean pop music (called K-Pop), and for Japan, the use of anime resulted in a sharp increase in individuals wanting to learn Japanese. However, for Mandarin, it was a smorgasbord of reasons. A few of these reasons include the following:

- The ability to establish friendships with a wide array of individuals from different cultural backgrounds. When learning Mandarin, you are not only allowing yourself to interact with those who are indigenous to Chinese speaking countries, but you are creating a sense of common ground for interaction with other international students who have also started to learn Mandarin. What many have done in order to strengthen the aptitude of their Mandarin language is look for a cross-language penpal. What you do is teach someone from China your indigenous language whilst they teach you theirs. They say that one of the best ways to learn a language is to converse with a local, and this is a mutually beneficial way to do just that.

- Many find that the language barrier present in other countries prevents them from visiting them. This is definitely the case in countries that have Mandarin as their official language. Therefore, it is human nature to want to overcome challenges that present themselves. This is why many take it upon themselves to learn Mandarin before either traveling or moving abroad. Not only does it make the entire experience easier, but it allows you more time to explore and delve even deeper into that country's culture (and this is time that would have been spent trying to figure out where to go next).

- Interest in Chinese drama shows has increased over the years. According to SHINE News, these Chinese drama shows (shortened to C-drama) have attracted so much popularity that they are now being streamed from Netflix, Hulu, and Amazon Prime. The show called *The Untamed* became a worldwide sensation, as there were people streaming from more than 200 countries, breaking all records within the Chinese drama industry. This has resulted in an increase in both professionalization and industrialization in the Chinese entertainment industry so as to cater to the growing international market.

Mandarin-speaking countries have always shown a need for international individuals to teach English within their schools and universities. The reason for this is to promote ease of communication with other countries. After all, English is seen as the standardized language of communication worldwide.

With that being said, many individuals obtain a basic bachelor's degree at a local university, then emigrate to a Mandarin-speaking country asan English teacher. While the salaries may seem rather small, one needs to take into consideration the very low standard of living in countrieslike China. This means that an individual will definitely be getting more bang for their buck.

To give you a little more insight, here are some of the expected earnings along with added benefits that one can expect when teaching English in China:

- Public schools: Salaries range from RMB 6,200 - 15,300 ($900 - $2,200). The benefits that come with this include working shorter hours in comparison to private schools, as well as having longer paid vacations. Most schools will offer teachers an option for free meals, which can be seen as a fantastic way to experience another country's food culture while saving money in the process.
- Private language academies: One can expect to earn RMB 6,200 - 16,000 ($900 - $2,300) per month. How this typically differs from public schools is that the salary earned is based on the amount of personal teaching experience you have, as well as the level of education that you have achieved. The curriculum at private academies tend to be more rigid than public schools, meaning that you will need to know a specific level of Mandarin in order to work at these institutions.
- Universities: In these pristine institutions, one can expect a salary of RMB 7,000 - 9,700 ($1,000 - $1,400). Along with this, typically there is a lighter workload and far fewer teaching hours when compared to other instructors. On top of the latter, those who teach English at universities also enjoy paid accommodation, free airfare, and more time to explore.
- International schools: These are where you want to teach as you will find the highest salaries. Expected salaries are RMB 11,800 - 29,000 ($1,700 - 4,300). However, landing one of these jobs is not only a lot more difficult, but there are sizably lower benefits and longer working hours.

Learning Mandarin before taking up a teaching position will enable you to adequately discuss the terms and conditions of your contract, as well as the benefits that come with it. You will also be able to establish relationships with your colleagues, providing a more comfortable working environment. Working abroad can make one feel rather alone, especially if you don't know anybody. Thus, being able to establish these relationships will also be beneficial for one's mental health.

Mandarin can be used to better understand your immediate environment as well. Whether you are in Singapore, mainland China, or Taiwan, it is likely that newspapers, news channels, and road signs will be in Mandarin. Thus, learning the language will result in fewer struggles as you begin to navigate your everyday life. The *Northwest Asian Weekly* has expressed the need for foreigners to actively read their country's respective newspapers. Not only does this create an understanding of current events, but it further allows one to develop an open and critical mind. Therefore, they recommend that one takes at least twelve months of intensive Mandarin classes before emigrating.

Obtaining adequate and correct healthcare also requires a small amount of language knowledge. Although most healthcare professionals are trained to converse with patients in both English and Mandarin, seeking and obtaining healthcare may prove to be very difficult if one cannot understand road signs or instructions indicating where to go.

Furthermore, many healthcare institutions only provide directions for how to take medications in Mandarin. Not understanding their diagnosis and the type of medication that is being given is worrisome and stress-inducing. *Psychology Today* has recorded that there is a 92% chance that an individual will default their treatment should they not understand how or why they are taking specific medication. Thus, in order to mitigate the chances of this occurring, a basic understanding of the Mandarin language should be obtained.

Mandarin is also used in promoting and reinforcing a form of cultural heritage among communities. With many different cultural events and festivals being based on historical teachings, the base tabloids that are kept in museums have more than likely been translated into traditional Chinese characters. Thus, in order to effectively understand the core of these cultural traditions and festivities, Mandarin needs to be understood. This means that by promoting a culture that focuses on learning Mandarin, the heart of specific cultures remains preserved.

A few examples of Chinese festivals and heritage days that have been preserved since before the Shang Dynasty which are still celebrated today include the following:

- Tomb Sweeping Day: A part of the Qingming (清明) festival, this day has been celebrated for more than 2,500 years. This is when people will show respect to their ancestors by cleaning their graves, offering food or wine, and burning incense. At these tombs, they also pray for their families and that their ancestors will continue to watch over them, keeping them safe and healthy.

- Dragon Boat Festival: Also known as the Duānwǔ Jié (端午节) Festival, it is a day of cultural prayer and worship honoring Qu Yuan, an exiled official who drowned in the Miluo River and whose body has never been recovered. Thus, every fifth day of the fifth lunar month, boats will be paddled out on a river to the sound of beating drums. This is with the main intent to keep fish and evil spirits away from Qu Yuan's body.

- Lantern Festival: Also known as Yuánxiāojié (元宵节), the Lantern Festival is a tradition that ends the Spring Festival (more specifically the Chinese New Year). For the past 2,000 years, lanterns have been lit as a way for people to pray for their futures. For example, women who would want to fall pregnant walk under a lantern that has the symbol of "baby" on it.

The Mandarin language has become ingrained in the societies of many countries, and learning the language has become necessary to navigate life within specific countries. However, it needs to be acknowledged that learning Mandarin is an ongoing process, requiring hours of dedicated studying and repetition. The amount of opportunities that learning Mandarin grants you with, however, knows no bounds and will only aid in your personal development.

Chapter 3:

How to Approach Learning

Mandarin – Studying Tips and

Tricks

At this point, you have already heard that learning Mandarin can be rather difficult. However, it is not knowing where to start learning that typically stops people from pursuing learning the language. One really needs to be sure that they are learning Mandarin for the right reasons, as passion fuels action; where there is no passion, there will be no action. Learning Mandarin is not for everyone, especially as it takes countless more hours to learn in comparison to other languages.

What is recommended is taking a free online class with either "Tutor Mandarin" or "eChinese Learning" to see if pursuing learning the language is right for you. Not only will you get a first-hand look at what learning it looks like, but you will get a feel as to how much time you will need to dedicate in order to truly learn the language.

Whether it be a personal goal or a rather impulsive want, it is advised to do some research on Mandarin learning materials that are available online. When it comes to learning the language, it is going to take a lot more than attending a few classes. Keats School and StudyCLI are two institutions that offer seminars, immersion programs and study abroad opportunities, which is perfect for anyone who wants to take their learning to the next level.

A resource that many recommend is called Fluenz. It allows you to consolidate the knowledge you have learned in online classes with the information that you are going to find in these two workbooks. The book that you are currently reading, as well as its associated counterpart, work perfectly with Fluenz, especially seeing as the amount of practice provided will have you reading and writing Mandarin in no time.

Make sure that you have a few notepads handy that you have dedicated solely to practicing your Chinese characters and pinyin. Preferably, try to pick a notebook that has large line spaces and margins as this will make jotting down characters that much easier while also providing more than enough space to practice the writing of the characters.

Learning pinyin will be the next step since it allows you to come to terms with how Mandarin words are pronounced and expressed using Chinese characters. With pinyin being the most commonly used system to learn written Chinese, it acts as a great introduction to the "one syllable" rule. This rule focuses on each Chinese character representing one syllable, which can be written out phonetically in pinyin. An example would be "wǒ shì zhōngguó rén" which has five syllables.

Thus, it is represented by five Chinese characters as 我是中国人. However, as you start to delve deeper into your studies, you will begin to realize that the pronunciation of pinyin is not as if you would read the word in English. An example of this is "shi", which is not pronounced as "she" but rather as "sure".

Once you have worked through the basics in this book and have a rather detailed notebook with all that you have learned, it is time to start speaking Mandarin to others. You will hear many saying that the best way to learn a language is to speak to a native speaker, and this is 100% true. With native speakers, they will be able to correct you regarding your pronunciation, allowing you to conceptualize where you are not pronouncing words correctly and rectify it before it becomes habitual. Conversing with a native speaker will also develop your confidence, allowing you to take your next step, which is constructing phrases from saying simple words.

You want to ensure that you are immersing yourself in the Mandarin language as often as possible, which is why listening to it during your morning commute is highly recommended. By doing so, you will begin to recognize sounds that go together and understand meaning in conversational Mandarin.

At the beginning, you may feel like they are speaking too fast, especially when you are listening to a news channel. However, you don't necessarily need to listen to the news; you could listen to a Mandarin podcast that teaches you a new Chinese character each day. This is why it is recommended to use "ChinesePod" to really maximize your learning. This becomes important when we start to look at the tones in Mandarin later on.

Many want the quickest route to learning Mandarin. This is why we decided to give you some studying tips and tricks to make your learning journey that much more exciting and fun. It is important that you are able to set both short-term and long-term goals, as this allows you to work toward something. For example, where do you want to be in terms of Mandarin fluency in three months, nine months, and one year? It is important to be realistic about these goals and base them off of how much time you are able to commit per week to learning Mandarin. As you move from your long-term goals to your short-term ones, set monthly goals that could vary from having memorized a hundred Chinese characters to even reading an easy Chinese book.

Also, make sure that these goals envelop the SMART criteria. This means the following:

- Specific (S): One wants to ensure that the goal that you have in mind is specific. Ask questions like, "What needs to be accomplished?", and, "What steps need to be taken to achieve this?" As you start to answer these questions, you are providing prompts that will ultimately establish a highly specific goal that is context-specific.
- Measurable (M): Adding numbers to your goal quantifies it, allowing it to be even more impactful. How many Chinese characters do you want to have memorized in two months? 30?

100? Being able to establish these small yet concise goals provides a newfound self-confidence that establishes a positive growth pattern as you continue to learn Mandarin.

- Attainable (A): When a goal is reached, it should empower you to take the next step, which is why you need to have a serious reality check. Is your goal realistic? One cannot expect to have a hundred Chinese characters memorized in one month when only one hour per week is spent actively studying.
- Relevant (R): The best goals have a benefit attached when achieving them. You want to really delve deep and establish why this goal is important to you. Will learning Mandarin give you improved education prospects? Will it allow you to create a better life for you or your family? As soon as you attach a benefit to your goal, you make it more real, with there being a tangible result that you can gain once completing it.
- Time-bound (T): If you don't have a deadline imposed on your goals, you are going to keep procrastinating and, in the end, not reaching them. This aspect of SMART provides deadlines for your goals. Your goals can also have mini checkpoints that are time-bound. For example, if you want to learn a hundred new Chinese characters per month, this means that you need to learn twenty-five new Chinese characters per week.

Reviewing your goals and ensuring that they remain SMART is the key to not only achieving your goals, but learning Mandarin at a pace that fits your routine and schedule. It is important that you are not afraid to alter your goals. It is better to be realistic about your capabilities— given all your other commitments—than needing to deal with the emotional turmoil of not achieving your goals at all. This is where you need to create a learning plan and study timetable to ensure that you do not fall behind.

It is vital that you do not only dedicate one time period a week to learn Mandarin, but instead make sure that there is a set time every day that you study. Not only will this result in you learning the content more quickly, but it will ensure that your foundation is strong. It is advised to focus on short sessions of study, as our brains work best in small spurts rather than long and ongoing study sessions.

By incorporating activities that combine speaking, writing, reading, and listening into your daily schedule, you will learn Mandarin at a faster pace. As you want to combine these skills, there are definite ways that they can be practiced. A few examples are as follows:

- Reading and speaking: The easiest and most cost-effective way to combine these two skills is by reading aloud. As you continue to do this, you will realize the importance of tones, as well as ensure that you acknowledge them in speech. This will also help you in hearing how you will sound when you talk to others. Many find it helpful to make flashcards that they use to practice when they are commuting or when they are in a line at the grocery store. Some find that it is useful to match the content of the flashcards to the activity that they are doing. For example, learning some breakfast foods while eating breakfast or some work-related terms when you are in the office are fantastic ways to provide context to what you are learning.
- Listening and writing: What many find to be of great use is listening to any Mandarin-speaking show on YouTube, and then having a friend who is fluent check if what you heard was correct or not. Not only does this increase your capacity to listen intently, but it also allows you to become accustomed to the speed at which conversational Mandarin occurs. Doing this for approximately 15 minutes per day is highly recommended.
- Reading and writing: Typically, people just starting their Mandarin studies will find this aspect rather mundane at first. However, it really is the best method to master those rather difficult Chinese characters. You will begin to notice that there are many characters that look similar, with very subtle differences providing an entirely different meaning. An easy

way to practise this is to read a sentence and then write it down. If you are a beginner, start off by writing the pinyin first followed by the corresponding Chinese characters below.

It is important that when you start learning Mandarin, even at the beginning phases, that you start to focus on phrases instead of the intricate nuances of individual vocabulary. Vocabulary is a crucial part to any language; however, one needs to ensure that there is context for the vocabulary to actually make sense. Try adding a phrase or sentence that uses a character that you have just learned. This ensures that you learn context, making it that much easier to use the content when having a conversation.

Remember, do not be daunted by the intricacies of Mandarin grammar. It is one of the last aspects that those learning Mandarin truly master, primarily because it comes with time. When learning them, make sure you fully understand one aspect before adding another. Otherwise, you will become confused by the very fine nuances and get frustrated.

If you find yourself to be a visual learner, we recommend the sticky note method of learning Chinese characters. Purchase a pack of different-colored sticky notes, letting each one represent a different category of words. Writing down characters and phrases onto these sticky notes and then putting them up on your wall will allow you to visualize the content more readily.

Furthermore, many find that putting the sticky notes on a wall near their door helps a lot. The reason for this is that they challenge themselves to learn or repeat a new Chinese character before they enter and exit the room. Thus, they are constantly interacting with the content, inadvertently including it as a part of their daily routine. If you cannot get a hold of colorful sticky notes, the same aspect can be applied using white one and an array of colorful pens.

Once you feel that you have started to get a grasp on the language, it is time to take the next big step. We call this "total immersion". What this encompasses is changing the language settings on your electronic devices to Mandarin so that you can learn to navigate the language in a hands-on manner. With this manner of learning, there can be both bouts of frustration as you cannot get where you need to go on your device and happiness as you successfully navigate your device. However, one needs to be sure that they are ready to undergo total immersion, because if not, it could result in an individual feeling intensely overwhelmed, to the point that one does not want to learn Mandarin anymore.

As you progress through your journey of learning Mandarin, you may find that the above tips and tricks may not necessarily work for you. However, that is the joy of learning a new language as you start to find what manners of learning really work for you. We are at the part of the book where you will begin to learn more about the practicalities of Mandarin, how to read it, as well as what some of the more common word choices are when speaking to friends, co-workers, and family.

The time to delve into learning Mandarin is now, so get your notebooks and pens ready as you physically begin your journey of adding another language to your repertoire.

Chapter 4:

Mandarin Character Uniqueness

Over 955 million people speak Mandarin as their mother tongue, surpassing English to be the most commonly spoken mother tongue in the world. Being the only modern pictographic language, Mandarin was developed using images, resembling a game of Pictionary. Almost all of the Mandarin characters are derived from actual historical images and objects. Let's take a look at the word "shan" which means "mountain".

Its character is 山, which looks like three points of a mountain range. With that being said, complicated characters that have up to 17 brush strokes are usually created by an amalgamation of smaller characters that build up to the overall character's meaning.

Typically, each individual character that makes up a more complex character is called a radical. An example of this is the word "feeling", which has 情 as its character. Now this character is comprised of three different radicals, as follows:

- Heart: 忄
- Plentiful: 丰
- Moon: 月

As we see that the combination of the above makes up the 情 character, as soon as you change any of these radicals, the entire meaning of the character will change. For example, if you were to change the "heart" radical you would be able to make 请 which means "to ask", and 清 which means "clear". This is where you are able to see the degree of character uniqueness that Mandarin shows. This does not mean that there has been no Western influence in some of the words adopted by Mandarin. A few examples are as follows:

- Amoeba: Āmǐbā (阿米巴)

- Bacon: Péigēn (培根)

- Bagel: Bèiguǒ (贝果)

- Chocolate: Qiǎo kè lì (巧克力)

- Coffee: Kā fēi (咖啡)

- Cookie: Qǔqí (曲奇)

- Golf: Gāoěrfū (高尔夫)

- Massage: Mǎshājī (马杀鸡)

- Sofa: Shā fā (沙发)

- Tuna: Tūnnáyú (吞拿鱼)

Each syllable in pinyin has a corresponding Chinese character. Thus, whenever you find yourself adding more pinyin to a sentence, you can expect additional characters to be written. This is how the "regular script" was defined during the Wei to Jin period. With regular script being attributed to Zhong Yao near the end of the Han Dynasty, he is typically known as the father of regular script. Having discussed him in a previous chapter, what we did not mention is that the earliest surviving pieces of regular script were, in fact, handwritten notes by Zhong Yao.

Having aided the development into dominant modern-day Mandarin script, a typical character is drawn today by using semi-cursive stroke, along with pauses to end horizontal strokes and heavy tails on strokes that are written in the downward-right diagonal.

It is because the characters are so unique that the task of memorizing them can seem rather tedious. However, to effectively tackle this challenge, we suggest adopting an eight-week studying timetable that focuses on learning radicals first before diving even deeper into the learning of Mandarin phrases. Here are a few examples of the radicals that one would typically find to the left of the Chinese character:

Radical	Radical as a character	Pinyin	Meaning	Examples
亻	人	Rén	Person	- You: nǐ(你) - They: tā men (他们)
氵	水	Shuǐ	Water	- River: hé (河) - Wash: xǐ (洗)
日	日	Rì	Time or Day	- Time: shí (时) - Early: zǎo (早)
女	女	Nǚ	Female	- Good: hǎo (好) - Mom: mā ma (妈妈)
月	月	Yué	Moon	- Wear: fú (服) - Friend: péng yǒu (朋友)
𧾷	足	Zú	Foot	- Kick: tī (踢) - Run: pǎo (跑)
扌	手	Shǒu	Hand	- Push: tuī (推) - Pull: lā (拉)

讠	言	Yán	Language	- Talk: shuō huà (说话) - Language: yú yán (语言)
口	口	Kǒu	Mouth	- Sing: chàng (唱) - Drink: hé (喝)
子	子	Zǐ	Child	- Child: hǎi zi (孩子) - Diligent: zī (孜)

The above is not an exhaustive list as there are also radicals that are present in other areas of the Chinese character. However, so as to not overload your brain, we will leave them out for now. There are more than 200 radicals in Mandarin, which means that even by learning two radicals per week, you are going to be studying them for quite some time. But why not have a little bit more fun with them by grouping them together based on commonality?

Remember, deciding to study Mandarin is not a quick fix to your desire to become a linguist. It is going to take a good couple of months, and even years, until you have mastery over the language. Having mentioned the eight-week program, here is an example that utilizes learning one radical per week:

- Week 1: Using the radical 人, focus on establishing a concrete foundation in your basic greetings and the use of pronouns. As using the correct pronoun shows a heightened level of respect when conversing with native speakers, ensure that you have a good understanding of it.

- Week 2: The radical 子 focuses on education and family, which require an understanding of the Week 1 radical in order to fully grasp the concepts of the Chinese characters.

- Week 3: It is highly likely that you will need to interact with a host family or a native speaker of Mandarin. This is why the radical 宀 is important this week, especially as it includes characters relating to "house" and "family".

- Week 4: Learning about how to communicate your level of Mandarin language capability, even if it is not much, is a fantastic way to let others know to simplify thoughts so you can understand them better. This is why focusing on the radical 言 is so important as it caters for all Chinese characters that have to do with "language".

- Week 5: You will most likely find yourself lost in a country where Mandarin is a native language. This is primarily because the road signs will only be in Mandarin. With that being said, this week you will need to focus on the 阝 radical, especially seeing as it refers to all characters that have to do with "directions".

- Week 6: Needing to move around a city is imperative. However, in order to do that, one needs to know the 辶 radical. This radical covers everything that has to do with "motion" and "transport".

- Week 7: The radical 疒 needs to be studied, especially if one must seek medical help. Referring to all characters related to "illnesses", it forms a core component of successfully being able to navigate life in a Mandarin-speaking country.

- Week 8: Being able to express yourself as well as your concerns is important. This is why characters regarding "thoughts" and "feelings" should be focused on during this week. The radical that you should look for is 忄.

One can think of a complex Mandarin character as a mathematics equation where the result is a character that has in-depth meaning. There are a bunch of resources available online that list the 200 radicals. Using the above method of practice, add and remove radicals to be studied that week as you see fit and based on your capabilities and available time.

What you further need to ensure is that you do not forget what you have learned in previous weeks, especially as some of the characters with specific radicals will begin to build on one another. This is why it is suggested to spend 30 to 45 minutes per day recapping what you have already learned, especially before you jump to the next week's content. Remember that adjusting your schedule does not mean that you are a failure but rather that you are cognizant of your own abilities and want to ensure that you fully understand the context of the content before moving on.

Chapter 5:

Tones

One thing that is imperative to your success in learning Mandarin is understanding the tonal aspects of the language. With many linguists believing that tones did not exist during the use of Old Chinese, they do play a vital component in differentiating the meaning of words. Tones exist when writing pinyin and need to be adhered to as missing a tone could change the entire context of a sentence. There are many ways to learn how to pronounce tones, but it is important that tones are learned and pronounced correctly in order to ensure the topic of a conversation is maintained.

There are four main tones in the Mandarin language. These are as follows:

- First tone: This tone is referred to as "ping" (平) and is typically pronounced at a level but higher pitch. Its accentuation on the letter in pinyin is ā.

- Second tone: When pronouncing this tone, start off at a lower pitch, rising to end at a slightly higher pitch. Referred to as "shang" (上), the accentuation on the letter in pinyin is á.

- Third tone: Probably one of the most difficult tones to master, this one will have you start at a neutral tone, dipping to a lower pitch and then rising back to where you initially started. It is seen as the "falling and rising" tone, referred to as "qu" (去). In pinyin, its accentuation is ǎ.

- Fourth tone: Starting from a pitch that is slightly higher than neutral, the spoken syllable moves strongly and quickly downward. Called "ru" (入), it is often compared to the forcefulness of reprimanding another person. Its pinyin accentuation is à.

To provide some context regarding how important tones are, below is a table where the pinyin uses the same lettering but has different tones:

Pinyin	Chinese character	Meaning
mā	媽/妈	Mother
má	麻	Hemp
mǎ	馬/马	Horse
mà	罵/骂	Scold

Learning tones is not going to be easy; it requires a lot of practice. You also need to allow time for your ear to become trained to hear the different tones. At the very beginning, you will start to hear and analyze every individual tone. However, as soon as there is a case where tones are juxtaposed one after another, it may be difficult to fully comprehend. Even though you can hear that there is a distinct difference, if asked to replicate or reproduce that specific tone, you will most likely not be able to do it. If you are able to cultivate a willingness to want to pronounce the different tones, no matter how difficult they may seem, then you are well on your way to mastering Mandarin.

Typically, especially when you have conversed quite a lot, there is the development of a "3-second memory". However, even after prolonged exposure, it is said that the memory of tones will only last three seconds. This is why there needs to be constant repetition regarding the initials, tones, and finals. There are specific "tone pair drills" that can be performed, and they are especially useful for getting accustomed to the tones that are juxtaposed.

A step-by-step process by which tone combinations should be tackled first is written below. It list starts with the easiest at the top, leading to the most difficult at the bottom:

- Tone 1 - Tone 1
- Tone 4 - Tone 4
- Tone 2 - Tone 4
- Tone 2 - Tone 2
- Tone 4 - Tone 2
- Tone 1 - Tone 4
- Tone 2 - Tone 3
- Tone 3 - Tone 3: There is an important rule regarding the positioning of two tone 3s next to each other. When this happens, the written pinyin will remain the same. However, regarding speech, the first tone 3 should be changed to a tone 2.
- Tone 1 - Tone 3
- Tone 2 - Tone 1
- Tone 3 - Tone 4
- Tone 3 - Tone 1
- Tone 1 - Tone 2
- Tone 4 - Tone 1
- Tone 4 - Tone 3
- Tone 3 - Tone 2

There will be times where you make tons of mistakes. These mistakes will even occur when you start to show tonal success when making a deliberate effort. This is to be celebrated, as it shows that you are one step closer to learning Mandarin. However, at the beginning of your language journey, you will most likely only be able to identify tones of pinyin that you have become well acquainted with. You will know that you are starting to progress when you are able to identify and imitate a tone on a new word that you have yet to learn.

Chapter 6:

Pinyin Pronunciation

Delving deeper into pinyin pronunciation, it is important to understand what pinyin is composed of. Typically, it will have three components. These are the initial, tone, and final. All three of these components need to be present in order for a Chinese character to be successfully represented by it. Not only that, but depending on the selection of initials, tones, and finals, the Chinese characters will be different.

In Mandarin, initials are also referred to as starting sounds. Typically, these cannot stand alone and need to be augmented or followed by a semivowel or final. Do not stress if this is yet to make sense as we are still going to delve into each respective component of pinyin before piecing everything together.

Below, you will be able to find the most common initials used in pinyin, as well as how they should sound. By merging this table with an online resource that verbally sounds it out, you will be able to make sense of them quicker and easier. The table of starting sounds is as follows:

b	Pronounced as in English, as in bed
pPron	unced as in English, as in pen
mPron	unced as in English, as in moon

f	Pronounced as in English, as in fool
d	Pronounced as in English, as in dirt
t	Pronounced as in English, as in turn
n	Pronounced as in English, as in no
l	Pronounced as in English, as in land
g	Pronounced as in English, as in gun
k	Pronounced as in English, as in king
h	Pronounced as in English, as in hand
j	Pronounced as in English, as in jean
q	Pronounced as "ch", as in cheese or change
x	Pronounced as "sh", as in shout or shin

Initials do not necessarily have to be single words. In Mandarin, there are initials that are a little bit more difficult to pronounce and consist of two letters. With these initials not being pronounced as they would be in English, they require a bit more practice. The *zh*, *ch*, *sh*, and *r* sounds are pronounced with your tongue curled up and touching your palate while pronouncing the sound. *Zh, ch,* and *sh* are essentially the same sound and pronunciation as *z, c,* and *s* respectively except, in the latter, the tongue is not curled. These can be rather tricky, so ensure that you spend as much time as necessary in order to really perfect these pronunciations.

Although these can stand alone without the need of a semivowel or final, they are written with an "i" at the end whenever they stand alone, though the "i" is silent.

zh	Tongue curled up, sounds like "ch" in English but has a more solid sound like the "ds" in buds
ch	Tongue curled up, sounds like "ch" in English but has a sharper sound like the "ts" in cats
sh	Tongue curled up, sounds like "sh" in English, as in shape
r	Tongue curled up, pronounced as in English, as in ring
z	Pronounced as tz, with a soft t
c	Pronounced as ts, as in cats
s	Pronounced as in English, like sin

Semivowels are seen as pieces of literature that exist in between a vowel and a consonant. Two of the most prudent examples in the English language are "w" and "y". However, when referring to Mandarin, there are some letters that can be used as either an initial, semivowel, or final. A few examples of these, as well as how they are pronounced, are as follows:

i	Pronounced as "ee", as in feel
u	Pronounced as "oo", as in fool
ü	Pronounced like the "ou" in you

However, seeing as semivowels can be present on their own (i.e., without an initial preceding it), they are able to be incorporated in normal Mandarin conversation. The only alteration is the manner by which the semivowels will be written. Seeing as the above semivowels can be used interchangeably as either initials or finals, there needs to be some way by which they are distinguished, especially when being used as a semivowel. Thus, the following changes are made when using a semivowel in isolation:

- When the semivowel "i" is used, it is written in pinyin as "yi".
- When the semivowel "u" is used, it is written in pinyin as "wu".
- When the semivowel "ü" is used, it is written in pinyin as "yu". What needs to be noted is that the umlaut falls away when the semivowel is used as a single entity.

Finals are the last part of pinyin that is necessary for it to be completely understood. Here, you will need to know that finals can be grouped with initials, augmented with a semivowel, or can stand on its own. The only exceptions to the rule where a final can stand on its own is with: ê, ei, and eng. Here are a few examples of finals that are able to stand alone.

a	Pronounced as "ah", as in ah!
o	Pronounced as "oe", as in toe
e	Pronounced as "uh", as in duh
ê	Pronounced as "eh", as in ten
ai	Pronounced as "ie", as in lie
ei	Pronounced as "ay", as in bay
ao	Pronounced as "ou", as in loud
ou	Pronounced as "oe", as in toe (same as the above "o")
an	Pronounced as "un", as in undo
en	Pronounced as "in", as in Finland
ang	Pronounced as "ung", as in sung
eng	Pronounced similarly to the above "en" but with the "ng" pronounced as in English, as in sing or fang

er	Pronounced as "ur", as in fur

The following table will provide some examples of finals that are grouped with initials or are appended with semivowels. Not only do these make unique sounds that need to be studied in detail, but they can often be confused with each other. This is why we recommend that you fully understand and have conceptualized one sound before moving on to the next.

Finals beginning with "i"			
	With initial	Without initial	
i+a	ia	ya	Pronounced as "ia" in media
i+ê	ie	ye	Pronounced as "ye" in yeah
i+ao	iao	yao	Pronounced as "yow" in yowl
i+ou	iou	you	Pronounced as "yo" in yo-yo
i+an	ian	yen	Pronounced like yen
i+en	in	yin	Pronounced as "een" in seen

i+ang	iang	yang	Pronounced like young
i+eng	ing	ying	Pronounced as "ing" in sing

Finals beginning with "u"			
u+a	ua	wa	Pronounced like "wa" in was
u+o	uo	wo	Pronounced like "wo" in world
u+ai	uai	wai	Pronounced like why
u+ei	uei	wei	Pronounced like weigh
u+an	uan	wan	Pronounced like one
u+en	uen	wen	Pronounced as "win" in wince
u+ang	uang	wang	Pronounced like "wan" but with the "ng" sound at the end
u+eng	ong	weng	With initial, it is pronounced as "ong" in song, but without initials, the "w" sound is also pronounced

Finals beginning with "ü"			
ü+ê	üe/un	yüe/yue	Pronounced like u-ye
ü+an	üan/un	yüan/yuan	Pronounced like u-when
ü+en	ün/un	yün/yun	Pronounced u-win
ü+eng	iong	yong	Pronounced as "yon" in yonder with the "ng" sound at the end

In some Mandarin texts, you may find that the umlaut of the ü has been omitted. This is completely normal. Seeing as it can be rather confusing in terms of pronunciation when the umlaut remains in many pinyin words, due to the commonality in speech, it is removed when written after "j", "q", "x", and "y". You will never find the semivowel "u" after any of these four initials.

Chapter 7:

Mandarin Character Brush Strokes

With Mandarin, there is always order to everything that is done. With that being said, when you start to practice drawing Chinese characters, you will need to do it in a specific order.

In this chapter, that order is going to be tackled, as well as the names of the different strokes. It will be important to learn the names of the strokes, especially when using more advanced Mandarin resources in the future. The reason for this is that they will assume that you already have the knowledge of what the stroke looks like from your beginner level classes. This is why, for ease of understanding, under each stroke, an explanation and picture has been included.

Types of Mandarin Brush Strokes

One of the simplest strokes is referred to as "héng" (横), and it is also the Chinese character for "one". Yī (一) is the name of the character for the number one. How one would typically draw this stroke is by placing the point of your brush on the left hand side, moving it from left to right in one swift motion. If you want to focus on the calligraphy aspect of the stroke, you will see that there are very evident areas of being pushed down at either end of the stroke. A visual representation is as follows:

Another simple brush stroke, which is literally the héng stroke propped onto its side, is the "shù" (竖) brush stroke. It is a vertical line that is typically combined with the héng brush stroke. The result of this is the Chinese character for the number ten, also referred to as "shí" (十). It is in this case that we need to take into consideration the order of strokes.

First, the horizontal stroke will be drawn, followed by shù. A fun fact regarding this character is that it resembles the Roman numeral ten (X) if it were to be placed at an angle. It can therefore be deduced that there is a possibility that both evolved from counting in tens, with a cross-stroke representing the completion of the group. When we look at the calligraphy of this character, the same rules apply for the héng stroke. The shù stroke will have the brush or pen pushed down slightly at the top (i.e., the start), and at the end, will be lifted off. A visual representation is as follows:

There are two diagonal strokes that are present as a component of many more complex Chinese characters. These two strokes are piě (撇) and nà (捺). Tackling piě first (the blue brush stroke in the image below), it is one of the brush strokes that makes up the character for "person", known in Mandarin as rén (人). Calligraphically, piě will always start at the top right. It then moves at an angle, down toward the bottom-left where the brush or pen will leave the paper. A visual representation is as follows:

The diagonal nà (represented as the blue stroke in the image below) brush stroke may or may not start in the middle of another stroke. However, in this example, the nà stroke will start in the middle of the piě stroke. It is when the piě stroke is combined with the nà stroke that the rén character is completed. This stroke, calligraphically, will always start at the top left and then angle downward to the bottom -right. As it leaves the paper, an impression of the brush or pen is to be made. A visual representation of this brush stroke is as follows:

There are many simple strokes in Mandarin. Another one of them is seen as a little dot, and it is referred to as "diǎn" (点) in Mandarin.

However, although it is seen as a small dot, it is a lot more than a very simple and quick up and down motion. Calligraphically, the brush or pen will be dragged to the right in a very slight manner. It will then be lifted to mimic a dot. An example of how this dot looks on characters is seen in blue below, but it can also be seen in the number six, known as "liù" (六). Referring to the number six character below, the diǎn is above the héng stroke. Typically, the diǎn will be drawn first, followed by héng, then lastly by piě and nà. This can be visually represented as follows:

Kicking everything up a notch, the next brush stroke is tí (剔). It is best seen by looking at the character for "I", known as "wǒ" (我). This is comprised of two different characters, "shǒu" (手) which stands for hand, and "gē" (戈) which represents a spear. However, focusing on shǒu, one can see the tí stroke. It is calligraphically represented by an upward movement that darts toward the right-hand side, being completed with a pointed end. This character is visually represented as follows:

In Mandarin, there is a concept known as the "composite stroke". This term refers to two different movements of brush strokes that are joined together without lifting the brush or pen. The stroke we will be focusing on is the heng gou (横钩) stroke. To see this stroke clearly, we will refer to the Chinese character for "write", called "xiě" (写). The heng gou stroke, which is drawn below in blue, is composed of a horizontal héng stroke followed by the hook, referred to as gōu. To calligraphically explain this entire character, we will break it down into segments. Reading the character from the top, one can see a vertical stroke first drawn, followed by the heng gou. Below, one can see the pictograph of a bird, representing that of a magpie. This character is visually represented as follows:

As héng can be adapted to form shù, heng gou can be adapted to form shu gou (竖钩). The downward shù stroke is terminated by a flick in order to give the hook-like appearance of gou. A Chinese character that consists of a shu gou, is "shǒu" (手), which stands for "hand". Describing the character below, it represents the lines that cross over the palm of a hand. The order in which these strokes are drawn are from top to bottom, with the shu gou stroke being drawn last. Keep in mind that this character is also the radical for wǒ that was discussed previously. The shu gou can be visually represented in blue as follows:

The gou hook can be added to a curved stroke, referred to as "wan". This will then result in the stroke you see below, called "wan gou" (弯钩). Calligraphically, the wan gou starts off at the top left, creating a curve that is first round then becomes vertical. It then ends in a hook as it states in his name. The wang gou forms an integral part of "gǒu" (note the different accent on the "u"), which means "dog" (狗). This character can be visually represented as follows:

When we look at the "wǒ" (我) character (the character for "I"), it does not only consist of a "tí" (剔) stroke. On its other side, there is a stroke known as "xie gou" (斜钩). How this segment of the character is calligraphically represented is by starting at the top, angling the brush or pen in a way that is curved toward the right-hand side. At the end, a hook is present. This is created by the brush or pen being lifted from the paper quickly as the brush or pen moves to the right. This character, with its xie gou segment in blue, can be visually represented as follows:

In terms of how horizontal a brush stroke goes, it not only depends on where the stroke starts, but also whether you are adding a hook onto the end or not. When we look at the horizontal ping stroke, it can be combined with a hook in order to create "ping guo" (平钩). The ping guo is seen specifically in the Chinese character for "heart", referred to as "xīn" (心). This character has three dots and is very common, specifically as it gives the addition of "emotion" onto a character. Examples of words that have characters that will contain the "heart" radical are anger, sadness, and longing. Calligraphically, the ping guo will start at the top and move straight down, curving to the right and ending in a hook. This can be visually represented in blue as follows:

Many a time, individual strokes can be combined to create a character that looks like a box. Often, there are two strokes that are used to create a right-angled stroke. The sharp turn that you see in blue below is called "zhé". This is combined with the two strokes joined by the sharp turn, with the result being "shu zhe" (竖折). This stroke tends to be drawn last, especially seeing as it needs to be justified in size based on the contents that exist within the box. Calligraphically, this stroke requires a very delicate hand. One needs to ensure that their technique can create a sharp turn that does not represent a curve. Effectively, one is able to visualize this stroke as a shù stroke that is followed by a héng stroke combined into a single action. The shu zhe can be seen in the character "yī" (医), which means "to cure or heal". A visual representation of this character is as follows:

There is a very typical box-shaped character that is incorporated in the word "mouth" called "kǒu" (口) in Mandarin. The stroke that we will be referring to in the below picture (represented in blue) is "heng zhe" (横折). This specific stroke is created by making a horizontal stroke to the right, followed by a pause, then going downward. The latter creates a stroke that is similar to shù. The radical that refers to kǒu is used readily in situations where speech or eating is described. The heng zhe stroke can be visually depicted as follows:

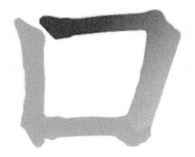

Now that you have a concrete understanding of basic brush strokes, as well as how they can link together, it is time to take it one step further. It is possible that three or more brush strokes can be combined in a variety of ways. One of these very common combinations is the "shu wan gou" (竖弯钩) stroke. This stroke follows the sequence of shù and wan, ending with a hooked gōu. This stroke is apparent in the Chinese character for "also", referred to as "yě" (也). Calligraphically, thisstroke is drawn by making a very short vertical line downward, curving to the right, and finishing with an upward flick. The latter represents the hook. The yě character is an important one to remember as it playsa part in the creation of characters for the personal pronouns "he" and "she". The shu wan gou stroke can be visually represented as follows:

Another very common combination of strokes is "pie dan" (撇点). This looks like a letter "V" that has been turned 90 degrees to the right. Calligraphically, it is a slanting stroke that begins at the top-right, meeting a center point then ending with a left slanting stroke. The pie dan stroke forms a part of the character "woman", known as "nǚ" (女). It is important to know the nǚ radical as it can have both negative and positive connotations. Negatively, it has been used in describing women as being jealous or angry, whereas on a more positive note this radical is also found in the characters for good and peace. The pie dan stroke can be visually represented in blue as follows:

The final example, where a series of strokes are combined together, is quite a complicated stroke. This stroke is called "shu zhe zhe gou" (竖折折钩). The key to understanding complex strokes it to break them down. When we break down shu zhe zhe gou, calligraphically, we will start with a shu stroke moving downward. This is then followed by two sharp turns (as indicated by zhe zhe), ending with a vertical hook. This stroke is typically seen in the Chinese character "horse", represented by "mǎ" (马). The shu zhe zhe gou stroke can be visually represented, in blue, as follows:

The Eight Brush Stroke Rules

When studying Mandarin, it is important that emphasis is placed on learning the sequences and directions that strokes should be drawn in. Not only will this ensure that you are able to draw Chinese characters correctly, but it will also save you time as you will become well accustomed to the steps necessary to correctly draw a character. As we look at examples of the eight different rules, remain cognizant that the deeper blue is the start of the stroke, with the gradient reaching a light blue in the direction that the stroke is going in.

The rules regarding brush strokes, are as follows:

- Rule 1: When drawing horizontal strokes, it is important to do so as the first stroke in a character. The reason for this is that they will often form the top of a Chinese character. To obey this rule, you will need to draw the stroke horizontally across and, only from there, move down if the character requires it. In the example below of shí, you can see that the rule is applied and followed.

- Rule 2: If you are faced with a character that consists of both piě and nà, the strokes are to be drawn from left to right. What this means is that the piě will need to be drawn first before nà. An example showing how the left falling, then right falling rule is obeyed can be seen with the Chinese character for "person", known as "rén" (人). This is as follows:

- Rule 3: Characters are to be drawn from top to bottom. Historically, the reason for this was to prevent smudging of the characters when the numbers one, two, and three were drawn calligraphically. The number three has three horizontal strokes which are drawn from top to bottom. The Chinese translation of the number three is "sān" (三). This rule and character can be depicted as follows:

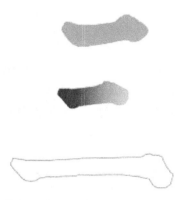

- Rule 4: Working from left to right, whilst following the previous brush stroke rules, is imperative in writing your Chinese characters correctly. With this being much easier for right-handed people, it may still take quite a bit of practice. A great example of working from left to right can be seen with the word "child", which is translated into Mandarin as "ér" (儿). This character, as well as the compliance to this rule, is depicted as follows:

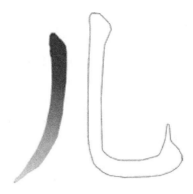

- Rule 5: Always work from the outside to the inside. This is of paramount importance when you are writing characters that have an outside box as you will need to ensure that there is more than enough space for the inner characters. An example of where this rule is used is the word "together", translated to Mandarin as "tóng"

(同). Remember that one will work from left to right, with the shù stroke (in brown) being drawn first, followed by the heng zhe gou stroke (in blue). This is diagrammatically depicted as follows:

- Rule 6: If the character has a completed box, the sealing stroke is done last. The reason for this is that it allows for the complete accommodation of all of the internal characters. Typically, the sealing stroke is a horizontal stroke that is drawn at the bottom of the character. The latter ensures that the rules already mentioned are being followed. To depict this, we will look at the word "country", translated into Madarin as "guó" (国). It is as follows:

- Rule 7: If you need to draw a character that has a central stroke that bisects the character, then it needs to be drawn before the left to right rule is applied. What this does is create symmetry for ease of reading and writing. An example of where this rule is applied is the word "small", translated to Mandarin as "xiǎo" (小). This central stroke is depicted, using xiǎo, as follows:

- Rule 8: A rule that is more focused on personal preference is the drawing of the character dots. Some people find it easier to draw the dots first as it provides them with a foundation for the construction of the rest of the character. Others find it easier to end with the dot. When we look at a rather common Chinese character, "de" (的), a possessive article, it seems that it would be simpler to draw the dot at the end. However, to reiterate, this is all based on personal preference. Here is a diagrammatic representation of where a dot can be situated:

Chapter 8:

What Can Go Wrong, and How

Can We Rectify It?

The world as we know it is becoming more interconnected. What this requires from us is the ability to adapt to these changes by learning different languages. Not only does learning a new language broaden our horizons, but it also increases our relationship circles as we have the capability to interact with a wider variety of people. When we learn another language, it requires effort, patience, and time. However, sometimes this is more difficult to achieve than we thought.

With that being said, we are going to tackle what could possibly go wrong while learning a new language, as well as what you can do to rectify these issues.

What Can Go Wrong?

Many times we remain transfixed in our errors that we tend to not be able to progress at the rate and pace that we would like. However, it is important to realize that you are not alone in this regard. It is common for individuals to feel stagnated when learning a new language, especially Mandarin. Before tackling what we can do to fix the problems, we need to first focus on what could go wrong.

Here are nine of the most common instances of what could go wrong, hindering your progress learning Mandarin. Take a look below.

1. Feeling discouraged by the mistakes that you make.

You need to remember that making mistakes is all part of the process. We can go even further to say that mistakes are important. Not only do they let you know where the gaps in your knowledge are, but they also create an additional learning opportunity for you to progress in Mandarin. As soon as you change your mindset so that mistakes are actually a fun part of the process, you will begin to see that the errors you are making are not as bad as they seem. It does not matter whether you are struggling with grammar, vocabulary, or character drawing— mistakes will happen. The quicker that you are able to deal with them, the better.

2. Not understanding the manner by which you learn.

How we decide to learn is just as important as the content that we are learning. One needs to understand what their learning style is, because the means by which we retain and interact with information is completely different. It is highly recommended that before you start studying Mandarin, you do a learning style test (there are many free ones online). Some of the questions they will ask may include, "Do you prefer reading about your interests over and above listening to them?", or, "Do you prefer a more hands-on approach when learning new concepts?" It is when you can understand yourself that you will be able to establish a tailored discipline toward learning and retaining what you learn during your journey.

3. Not starting off with the sounds.

One of the first concepts that one should focus on when learning a new language is sounds. With so many individuals not starting this way, they are already creating an unstable foundation, as well as more difficulty in learning Mandarin. You may feel the need to jump straight to reading and writing Mandarin, but how will you know if your pronunciation is correct without having studied the sounds? Verbal exercises are pivotal when learning Mandarin, especially because of the little nuances that are associated with the different tones in the language. By not starting with this first, you are already putting yourself at a disadvantage.

4. *Your main focus is on the incorrect vocabulary.*

One needs to be cognizant of the words that they are feeding their brain, especially at the beginning stages of learning a new language. Mandarin possesses such a wide variety of different categories, which can make it seem rather difficult when needing to choose which ones to focus on. When referring to Mandarin, learning the numbers, colors, vehicles, different types of food, and family members are good places to start. The words in these categories are simple enough to get you conversing with others, as well as diverse enough in order to ensure that you are practicing all the sounds necessary as a beginner.

5. *Poor construction of sentence vocabulary.*

Building sentences is a basic piece of learning another language, and it is frequently disregarded. There are a key amount of expressions that many beginners in Mandarin learn, especially if they want to travel to a country where Mandarin is the native language.

In English, a few of these expressions incl ude the following: "Hi", "Farewell", "I apologize", and "Thank you". Learning these common expressions will help you grasp the context of Mandarin faster while also building confidence for when you speak to native speakers. If you do not focus on these important Mandarin expressions, you will most likely feel less confident in your speaking abilities. This will further result in you not being able to be corrected by others, ultimately slowing down the learning process.

When you start constructing basic sentences, it is important that you start to use simple verbs. Referring to these different verbs, there are numerous examples in the next chapter. It is when you begin to realize that the simple and basic sentences become easier that you can start to learn more complex phrases.

6. *Fixating too much on grammar.*

When you start learning Mandarin, it is important that you do not fixate too much on the grammar. It is when you start getting caught in the confusion of grammar that your focus shifts from learning the basics to wanting to become too good too fast. Grammar lessons will come later, and in terms of Mandarin, not learning it immediately will not hinder your progress in learning the language.

7. *Worrying too much on pronunciation.*

Remember that many who want to learn Mandarin wish to be perfect at it. It is when one becomes stagnated in wanting to be perfect in one's pronunciation, that progression is hindered. It can become extremely frustrating when you already speak a language that has its own tones. In this case, when you learn Mandarin, you might want to make the distinction in pronunciation as clear as possible. If you find yourself struggling with pronunciation, do not stress.

This is one of the first hurdles that you will need to overcome. The more that you practice a language, the more accustomed you will get to the unique sounds. Try your best to speak to native Mandarin speakers as much as possible, as they will be more than willing to point out errors in your pronunciation. It is important to understand that corrections in pronunciation are not a personal attack, but just natives who want you to succeed in learning Mandarin.

8. *Listening to native speakers too soon.*

One of the first tests to see how far you have progressed in learning Mandarin is to try your skills by speaking with a native speaker. However, if you start to speak to a native speaker too soon, there is a large chance that there will be a major drop in your morale if you do not succeed as well as you would have hoped to. Instead of only focusing on speaking, try intently listening to the native speakers talk. It is okay to not be able to understand what native speakers are saying. However, allow yourself the time to learn instead of feeling upset. Learning Mandarin is not a race; it is a journey.

9. Not being in the correct mindset.

We need to remember that we all live our own lives. On some days, we will be in the mood to learn Mandarin, and on other days, not so much. However, we cannot let one instance dictate our progress, especially when it comes to Mandarin. After all, it is a language that needs daily study, and if you are in the incorrect mindset for one day and do not study, you may throw yourself completely out of your routine. This may even result in giving up on learning Mandarin completely. What can be recommended is to give yourself a little pep talk when you do not feel like studying Mandarin that day. Reminding yourself of why you are studying Mandarin can also be a good method for shifting your mindset toward a more positive one.

What Can I Do to Fix It?

Sometimes you may feel hopeless as you have made an error that you just cannot fix. Unfortunately, these mistakes tend to happen more often than we think, especially when learning Mandarin. There will be times when you make either a vocabulary or even a stylistic error. Adults tend to feel embarrassed when they make a seemingly "silly" mistake. This degree of embarrassment knows no bounds, especially when they see children who are native speakers not making those errors.

When one makes a mistake, they tend to overthink absolutely everything. They even start to doubt their own abilities to learn

Mandarin. It is when mistakes start to be made during the studying process that most Mandarin language students will choose to give up. A student who cannot speak out about their teachings will not progress, primarily due to the fear or judgment that is expected.

Psychologist Lev Vygotsky believed that those who succeed were those who failed the most. This is what you need to come to terms with as you study Mandarin. The biggest error you can make is not making any mistakes at all.

Previously, everything that could go wrong when studying Mandarin was listed. However, what can we do about it? Here are seven ways to embrace the mistakes that you learn as you study Mandarin:

1. Drop your ego.

If you have an ego, it is important that you come to terms with learning to let go of it. It really does not matter who you are. The fact is that you are on the same playing field as everyone else who is wanting to learn Mandarin. Thus, if you are the CEO of a successful company or still living in the basement of your parents, you are a person who is going to most likely make mistakes as you learn Mandarin. It is important that you start to integrate yourself into online groups with people who are at the same learning stage as you. This will heighten your accountability with each other, as well as provide you with others to practice your language skills with.

If you find yourself uncomfortable in conversation, lean on your emotions rather than your ego. Start by letting the other person know that you are still learning the language, and so to not speak fast. Start by smiling, apologizing, and then informing them that you are trying your best to study Mandarin and are fully aware that it's not perfect.

Refer to the workbook, where we will be discussing a few of the phrases that you can use. When you admit that you are not perfect, others will understand and appreciate the effort that you are making in learning their language, even if your language use is riddled with mistakes.

2. Try not to compare yourself to others.

One of the worst things you can do is compare yourself to someone else who speaks your target language better than you do. It is even worse when you find yourself comparing your progress to native speakers or advanced learners. By now, you know that Mandarin has a smorgasbord of nuances that make it an intricate and rather difficult language to master. This means that you are going to want to spend a lot of time on repetition, time which others may have more of. It is because everyone has different lives and lifestyles that their Mandarin language journeys will be different.

Some people are natural extroverts, so speaking comes more natural to them than with an introvert. Others may be good with listening. Some who start learning Mandarin may have a rather musical ear, meaning that the nuances regarding pronunciation can be picked up a lot easier, while others may find it difficult to really hear the subtle differences in the tones of Mandarin pronunciation. Some find it easier to study in groups online, and others prefer one-on-one lessons that are in person.

Each individual has their own unique journey that's based on not only their personalities, but also their current life circumstances. It is in this way that you should use your learning style to your advantage, making it the core of how you approach your Mandarin studies. Imitating another person's learning style will only provide you with ineffective study sessions, setting you even further back. However, do not completely cut yourself off from the study methods of others, as you could always learn something new.

Know yourself and what works for you, as well as what does not. Remember, you are not other people, and your life is not theirs to live. After all, there are those who would never envision learning another language, so you are already one step ahead!

3. Converse with yourself in your target language.

Self-confidence is imperative when learning a new language. Many will tell you that talking to yourself could be seen as rather weird, but in this case, it is a way to become even more comfortable with speaking Mandarin. It does not matter if you are washing your car, making dinner, or feeding the dogs—challenge yourself to speak to yourself within the context of the action that you are doing.

This is an even better way of overcoming a possible fear of speaking in public, especially if you have anxiety revolving around being embarrassed if you were to make a mistake. What is suggested to do in Mandarin is explore the pros and cons, as well as what your dreams, aspirations, fears, and concerns are. You will find that you are your own best listener. The monologues that you will end up having with yourself are fantastic ways to train, especially when one of your end goals is to be able to talk to people. The more often you talk to yourself, the more you will start to understand your own language imperfections, being able to rectify them as quickly as possible.

4. Learn from your mistakes.

In order for you to overcome any form of fear related to speaking Mandarin, you will need to understand the mistakes that you have made, as well as systematically work through each one.

In Mandarin, there are typically two cases in which mistakes will be made. These are listed below:

- You make mistakes because you do not know something.
- You make mistakes because you cannot remember something that you have previously learned.

If you were able to identify your mistakes as fitting the first case, then your solution is to identify what knowledge you are lacking, then learn it. The mistake that you're making could be a grammatical rule that you have yet to study, a word that you are unfamiliar with, or even the mispronunciation of a word's tone, altering the entire word's meaning. The latter is a very common occurrence for those who are learning Mandarin.

So how do you fix this issue? Well, you grab your textbook or dictionary. Studying with a teacher would also prove beneficial in this case as they can directly help you identify any gaps that you have in your knowledge, suggesting ways to fix them.

In the situation where you have forgotten concepts and/or words that you had known before, the solution is to continue practicing. Remember that when you find yourself erroneously using a specific tone, or you forget a word when it comes to using it, it does not have any representation of your intelligence level. The fact that you were able to identify a possible problem shows that you are cognizant about your own progress.

If you find yourself repetitively forgetting a specific word, write it down on a flashcard, and whenever you find yourself with some time to spare, go over all the words you keep forgetting.

5. Take it step by step.

It is always important to note that people who speak a language fluently did not wake up one morning and have the entire language and all the Mandarin characters memorized. They had to learn it, and it took time. It is important that you stop judging yourself so harshly, and instead, allow yourself to only be where you are meant to be.

An example of this is a beginner in Mandarin who is not used to making the tones of the new language. Do not expect yourself to have perfect pronunciation, as it takes improving a little each and every day to reach that level. As you move from the beginner phase of Mandarin to the intermediate phase, you will not make fewer mistakes, you will just make more complex ones.

You need to remind yourself that the next step will always encompass learning more and getting into a bit more detail. However, you need to find time within these steps to be proud of how far you have already come. One needs to learn to accept and revel in the little wins, especially once they complete one step and are ready to move on to the next one. This strengthens one's confidence as they begin to realize that they are capable of learning Mandarin.

6. *Focus on your communication skills.*

It does not matter whether you find yourself speaking to a friend, a co-worker, or a native speaker of Mandarin—focus on what you are trying to say at that moment. As soon as you allow your mind to drift, you will lose your train and thought, with the result being ineffective communication. It is important to always do your best so that you can remain confident in your capabilities. The task that you have when communicating is not to sound perfect when doing so, but rather to ensure that you get your message across.

Your sentence structure can be riddled with mistakes, but if you were successfully able to relay your thoughts, your objective has been met. It is at this point that you should celebrate, because you have taken one more step in becoming fluent in Mandarin.

Ensure that you are working on your communication skills in your own time. However, it is important that you do not let your mistakes hinder your progress of completing real tasks in Mandarin. You will find yourself in a cycle that consists of two parts: learn and apply. You will learn a new Mandarin phrase, apply it to a conversation that you are having, and then look for the next phrase to learn or build an already existing one.

7. *Confide in yourself.*

Your brain is an organ that should be marvelled, especially since it remembers stored information that you believe you had forgotten.

Often, when we learn Mandarin, we get angry for not remembering one character. It is not the fact that we have forgotten all about it, but that it is just in that moment that we cannot remember it. This is when we need to allow our brains to take control, trusting ourselves in the process. Mandarin is not easy, but we forget that we have a brain that makes the seemingly impossible possible. You will find yourself feeling awestruck by its capabilities when you remember the word that you could not recall that morning whilst lying peacefully in your bed.

When you decide to put the effort and work into learning Mandarin, you will find that not only will you begin to trust yourself more, but you will start making fewer mistakes than you are used to. It is when we are in a stressed state that we freeze up, making errors that we would not typically make. This is why it is important to acknowledge your own abilities and how far you have come in already learning Mandarin. You must also trust the process.

A fear of making mistakes is what is going to be holding you back from perfecting your speaking skills. These fears need to be dealt with in a calm, collected, and healthy manner, or the repercussions could end up hindering your Mandarin progress even more.

Chapter 9:

Learning Some Words

By now, you have a strong foundation regarding how tones work, how to draw pinyin, as well as how to approach your Mandarin studies. Now it is time to apply some elbow grease as you start to learn some categories of Mandarin words.

Below, you will find some of the most commonly used terms that are most likely to come up in conversation. This is not an exhaustive list. However, if you find a word that is not in a category that it should be, write it in and start to create your own collection of Mandarin words.

Pronouns and Genders

Pronouns		
I, Me	我	Wǒ
You	你	Nǐ
You (formal)	您	Nín
Him, he	他	Tā

Her, she	她	Tā
It	它	Tā
Him, Her (godly/divine beings)	祂	Tā
It (animals)	牠	Tā
Plural pronoun		
Us	我们	Wǒmen
Them	他们	Tāmen
You guys	你们	Nǐmen
Possessive pronoun		
Mine	我的	Wǒ de
Ours	我们的	Wǒmen de
Yours	你的	Nǐ de

Yours (plural)	你们的	Nǐmen de
His	他的	Tā de
Hers	她的	Tā de
Theirs	他们的	Tāmen de
Its	它的	Tā de

Reflective pronouns		
Myself	我自己	Wǒ zìjǐ
Yourself	你自己	Nǐ zìjǐ
Himself	他自己	Tā zìjǐ
Herself	她自己	Tā zìjǐ
Itself	它自己	Tā zìjǐ

Genders		
Male	男	Nán

Female	女	Nǚ
Male animal	公	Gōng
Female animal	母	Mǔ

Greetings and Saying Farewell

Hello	你好	Nǐhǎo
Hello (formal)	您好	Nínhǎo
How are you?	你好吗？	Nǐhǎo ma
I am good	我很好	Wǒ hěnhǎo
Thank you	谢谢	Xièxiè
And you?	你呢	Nǐne?
How have you been?	你最近好吗？	Nǐ zuìjìn hǎo ma

Long time no see/it has been a while	好久不见	Hǎojiǔ bùjiàn (the bù is read as bú）
Good morning	早安	Zǎo ān
Good afternoon	午安	Wǔ ān
Good evening/good night	晚安	Wǎn'ān
Pleased to meet you	幸會 /高兴认识你	Xìng huì/ Gāoxìng rèn chí nǐ
Goodbye/see you again	再见	Zàijiàn
Let us meet soon	我们再约	Wǒmen zài yuē
I'm off/I'm leaving	我走了	Wǒ zǒule

Family Members

Mom	妈妈	Māmā
Mother	母亲	Mǔqīn
Dad	爸爸	Bàba
Father	父亲	Fùqīn
Husband	老公/丈夫	Lǎogōng/zhàngfū
Wife	老婆/妻子	Lǎopó/qīzi
Son	儿子	Érzi
Daughter	女儿	Nǚ'ér
Son-in-law	女婿	Nǚxù
Daughter-in-law	媳妇	Xífù
Child	孩子	Háizi

Older brother	哥哥	Gēgē
Younger brother	弟弟	Dìdì
Older sister	**姊姊**	Jiě jie
Younger sister	妹妹	Mèi mei
Grandfather (father's side)	爷爷	Yéyé
Grandfather (mother's side)	外公	Wàigōng
Grandmother (father's side)	奶奶	Nǎinai
Grandmother (mother's side)	外婆	Wàipó
Aunt (father's side)	姑姑	Gūgū
Uncle (father's brother-in-law)	姑丈	Gūzhàng
Aunt (mother's side)	阿姨	Āyí
Uncle (mother's brother-in-law)	姨丈	Yízhàng
Uncle (father's older brother)	伯伯	Bóbo

Aunt (father's older sister-in-law)	伯母	Bómǔ
Uncle (father's younger brother)	叔叔	Shūshu
Aunt (father's younger sister-in-law)	婶婶	Shěnshen
Uncle (mother's brother)	舅舅	Jiùjiu
Aunt (mother's sister-in-law)	舅妈	Jiùmā
Cousin (older male paternal cousin)	堂哥	Táng gē
Cousin (older female paternal cousin)	堂姐	Táng jiě
Cousin (younger male paternal cousin)	堂弟	Táng dì
Cousin (younger female paternal cousin)	堂妹	Táng mèi
Cousin (older male maternal cousin)	表哥	Biǎo gē

Cousin (older female maternal cousin)	表姐	Biǎo jiě
Cousin (younger male maternal cousin)	表弟	Biǎo dì
Cousin (younger female maternal cousin)	表妹	Biǎo mèi
Grandson (from son)	孙子	Sūnzi
Granddaughter (from son)	孙女	Sūnnǚ
Grandson (from daughter)	外孙	Wàisūn
Granddaughter (from daughter)	外孙女	Wàisūnnǚ
Nephew (from brother)	侄子	Zhízi
Nephew (from sister)	侄子	Zhínǚ
Niece (from brother)	外审	Wài shěn
Niece (from sister)	外审女	Wài shěn nǚ

Verbs

Accept	接受	Jiēshòu
Add	增加	Zēngjiā
Admire	欣赏	Xīnshǎng
Apologize	道歉	Dàoqiàn
Ask	问	Wèn
Become	成为	Chéngwéi
Believe	相信	Xiāngxìn
Bring	带	Dài
Borrow	借	Jiè
Buy	购买/买	Gòumǎi/mǎi
Change	更改	Gēnggǎi
Choose	选择	Xuǎnzé

Climb	爬	Pá
Complete	完成	Wánchéng
Cry	哭	Kū
Decide	决定	Juédìng
Deny	拒绝	Jùjué
Dream	梦想	Mèngxiǎng
Drink	喝	Hē
Drive (car)	开 (车)	Kāi (chē)
Eat	吃	Chī
Enjoy	享受	Xiǎngshòu
Examine	检查	Jiǎnchá
Explain	说明	Shuōmíng
Fall	摔倒	Shuāi dǎo

Feel	感觉	Gǎnjué
Fly	飞	Fēi
Forget	忘记	Wàngjì
Get	得到	Dédào
Give	给	Gěi
Hide	躲	Duǒ
Hit	打	Dǎ
Hug	拥抱	Yǒngbào
Introduce	介绍	Jièshào
Jog	慢跑	Mànpǎo
Joke	开玩笑	Kāiwánxiào
Jump	跳	Tiào
Kick	踢	Tī

Kiss	吻	Wěn
Laugh	笑	Xiào
Leave	离开	Líkāi
Look	看	Kàn
Meet	遇到	Yù dào
Need	需要	Xūyào
Open	打开	Dǎkāi
Pay	付	Fù
Practice	练习	Liànxí
Prepare	准备	Zhǔnbèi
Push	推	Tuī
Quit	放弃	Fàngqì
Read	读	Dú

Relax	放松	Fàngsōng
Remember	记得	Jìdé
Run	**跑**	Pǎo
Say	说	Shuō
Sell	卖	Mài
Sing	唱	Chàng
See	看	Kàn
Speak	说话	Shuōhuà
Stand	站	Zhàn
Study	读书	Dúshū
Take	拿	Ná
Think	想	Xiǎng
Try	试	Shì

Understand	理解	Lǐjiě
Wait	等待	Děngdài
Walk	走	Zǒu
Wash	洗	Xǐ
Write	写	Xiě

Numbers

Zero	零	Líng
One	一	Yī / Yāo
Yāo is mainly used when reading out phone numbers or sequence of numbers.		
Two	二 / 兩	Èr/liǎng
Èr is used when saying 2 or 20, but from the hundreds upward, liǎng is used. Èr is also used when referring to positioning, i.e., second place 第二名 (Dì èr míng).		

Three	三	Sān
Four	四	Sì
Five	五	Wǔ
Six	六	Liù
Seven	七	Qī
Eight	八	Bā
Nine	九	Jiǔ
Ten	十	Shí
Eleven	十一	Shí yī
Twelve	十二	Shí èr
Twenty	二十	Èr shí
Twenty-one	二十一	Èr shí yī
Thirty	三十	Sān shí

Hundreds	百	Bǎi
One hundred	一百	Yībǎi
One hundred and five	一百零五	Yībǎi líng wǔ
One hundred and ten	一百一十	Yībǎi yīshí
One hundred and forty-three	一百四十三	Yībǎi sì shí sān
Two hundred	二百	Liǎng bǎi
Twohundredand twenty-two	兩百二十二	Liǎngbǎi Èrshí'èr
Two hundred and fifty six	兩百五十六	Liǎngbǎi Wǔshíliù
Thousands	千	Qiān
One thousand	一千	Yì qiān
Two thousand	兩千	Liǎng qiān

Ten thousand	万	Wàn
Hundred-thousand	十万	Shí wàn
Million	百万	Bǎi wàn
Hundred-million	亿	Yì
Trillion	兆	Zhào

Animals

Animals	动物	Dòngwù
Ant	蚂蚁	Mǎyǐ
Baboon	狒狒	Fèifèi
Bat	蝙蝠	Biānfú
Bear	熊	Xióng
Bee	蜜蜂	Mìfēng
Bird	鸟	Niǎo
Buffalo	水牛	Shuǐniú
Butterfly	蝴蝶	Húdié
Camel	骆驼	Luòtuó
Cat	猫	Māo
Caterpillar	毛毛虫	Máo máo chóng

Cheetah	猎豹	Lièbào
Chicken	鸡	Jī
Cow	牛	Niú
Crab	螃蟹	Pángxiè
Cricket	蟋蟀	Xīshuài
Crocodile	鳄鱼	Èyú
Deer	鹿	Lù
Dog	狗	Gǒu
Dolphin	海豚	Hǎitún
Donkey	驴	Lǘ
Dove	鸽子	Gēzi
Duck	鸭子	Yāzi
Eagle	老鹰	Lǎoyīng

Elephant	大象	Dàxiàng
Fish	鱼	Yú
Fly	苍蝇	Cāngyíng
Fox	狐狸	Húlí
Frog	青蛙	Qīngwā
Goat	山羊	Shānyáng
Hawk	老鹰	Lǎoyīng
Horse	马	Mǎ
Impala	黑斑羚	Hēi bān líng
Kangaroo	袋鼠	Dàishǔ
Leopard	豹	Bào
Lion	狮子	Shīzi
Lizard	蜥蜴	Xīyì

Lobster	龙虾	Lóngxiā
Monkey	猴子	Hóuzi
Mosquito	蚊子	Wénzi
Moth	蛾	É
Mouse	老鼠	Lǎoshǔ
Octopus	章鱼	Zhāngyú
Ostrich	鸵鸟	Tuóniǎo
Owl	猫头鹰	Māotóuyīng
Panda	熊猫	Xióngmāo
Peacock	孔雀	Kǒngquè
Penguin	企鹅	Qì'é
Pig	猪	Zhū
Pigeon	鸽子	Gēzi

Rabbit	兔子	Tùzǐ
Salmon	三文鱼	Sānwènyú
Shark	鲨鱼	Shāyú
Sheep	羊	Yáng
Snail	蜗牛	Wōniú
Spider	蜘蛛	Zhīzhū
Tiger	老虎	Lǎohǔ
Whale	鲸鱼	Jīngyú
Wolf	狼	Láng
Zebra	斑马	Bānmǎ

Body Parts

Head	头	Tóu
Face	脸	Liǎn
Eyebrow	眉	Méi
Eyes	眼睛	Yǎnjīng
Nose	鼻子	Bízi
Ears	耳朵	Ěrduǒ
Mouth	口	Kǒu
Teeth	牙齿	Yáchǐ
Tongue	舌	Shé
Nostrils	鼻孔	Bíkǒng
Hair	头发	Tóufǎ
Beard	胡子	Húzi

Neck	颈部	Jǐng bù
Throat	喉	Hóu
Shoulders	肩膀	Jiānbǎng
Arms	手臂	Shǒubì
Elbow	手肘	Shǒuzhǒu
Wrist	手腕	Shǒuwàn
Hand	手	Shǒu
Fingers	手指	Shǒuzhǐ
Nails	指甲	Zhǐjiǎ
Palm	手掌	Shǒuzhǎng
Chest	胸部	Xiōngbù
Abdomen	腹部	Fùbù
Hip	臀部	Túnbù

Waist	腰部	Yāobù
Legs	腿	Tuǐ
Thighs	大腿	Dàtuǐ
Calves	小腿	Xiǎotuǐ
Knee	膝盖	Xīgài
Ankle	脚踝	Jiǎohuái
Feet	脚	Jiǎo
Toes	脚趾	Jiǎozhǐ
Brain	脑	Nǎo
Lungs	肺	Fèi
Heart	心	Xīn
Stomach	胃	Wèi

Intestines	肠子	Cháng zi
Liver	肝	Gān
Kidneys	肾脏	Shènzàng
Bladder	膀胱	Pángguāng
Arteries	动脉	Dòng mài
Veins	静脉	Jìngmài

Plants and Nature

Tree	树	Shù
Leaf	叶	Yè
Branch	科	Kē
Trunk	树干	Shùgàn
Roots	树根	Shùgēn

Flower	花	Huā
Petal	花瓣	Huābàn
Thorn	刺	Cì
Grass	草	Cǎo
Rose	玫瑰	Méiguī
Orchid	兰花	Lánhuā
Chrysanthemum	菊花	Júhuā
Sunflower	向日葵	Xiàngrìkuí
Lavender	薰衣草	Xūnyīcǎo
Cactus	仙人掌	Xiānrénzhǎng
Moss	苔藓	Táixiǎn
Vines	葡萄藤	Pútáo téng
Ground	地	Dì

Soil	土	Tǔ
Water	水	Shuǐ
Air	空气	Kōngqì
Sun	太阳	Tàiyáng
Clouds	云	Yún
Sky	天空	Tiānkōng
Star	星星	Xīngxīng
Moon	月亮	Yuèliàng
Sea	海	Hǎi
Ocean	海洋	Hǎiyáng
Waves	波浪	Bōlàng
Beach	海滩	Hǎitān
Sand	砂	Shā

Stone	石头	Shítou
Rain	雨	Yǔ
Fog	雾气	Wùqì
Dew	露水	Lùshuǐ
Smoke	烟	Yān
Mountains	山脉	Shānmài
Hills	山丘	Shānqiū
Forest	森林	Sēnlín
Fire	火	Huǒ
Cave	洞穴	Dòngxué
Desert	沙漠	Shāmò

Fruits, Vegetables, Nuts, and Grains

Fruit	水果	Shuǐguǒ
Vegetables	蔬菜	Shūcài
Nuts	坚果	Jiānguǒ
Grains	谷类	Gǔlèi
Apple	苹果	Píngguǒ
Banana	香蕉	Xiāngjiāo
Lemon	柠檬	Níngméng
Mango	芒果	Mángguǒ
Kiwi	奇异果	Qíyì guǒ
Pear	梨	Lí
Apricot	杏子	Xìngzi
Avocado	鳄梨	È lí

Blueberry	蓝莓	Lánméi
Cherry	樱桃	Yīngtáo
Coconut	椰子	Yēzi
Grapes	葡萄	Pútáo
Guava	番石榴	Fān shíliú
Honeydew	蜜瓜	Mì guā
Lychee	荔枝	Lìzhī
Papaya	番木瓜	Fān mùguā
Passionfruit	百香果	Bǎixiāng guǒ
Peach	桃子	Táozi
Pineapple	菠萝	Bōluó
Plum	李子	Lǐzǐ
Pomegranate	石榴	Shíliú

Strawberry	草莓	Căoméi
Tomato	番茄	Fānqié
Watermelon	西瓜	Xīguā
Beetroot	红菜头	Hóng cài tóu
Bell pepper	灯笼椒	Dēnglóng jiāo
Broccoli	西兰花	Xī lánhuā
Cabbage	卷心菜	Juǎnxīncài
Carrots	萝卜	Luóbo
Cauliflower	菜花	Càihuā
Celery	芹菜	Qíncài
Chilli	辣椒	Làjiāo
Cucumber	黄瓜	Huángguā
Eggplant	茄子	Qiézi

Garlic	大蒜	Dàsuàn
Ginger	生姜	Shēngjiāng
Green peas	青豆	Qīngdòu
Kale	羽衣甘蓝	Yǔyī gānlán
Lettuce	生菜	Shēngcài
Mushrooms	蘑菇	Mógū
Olives	橄榄	Gǎnlǎn
Onion	洋葱	Yángcōng
Potato	土豆	Tǔdòu
Pumpkin	南瓜	Nánguā
Radish	萝卜	Luóbo
Spinach	菠菜	Bōcài
Spring onion	葱	Cōng

Sweet potato	红薯	Hóngshǔ
Sweetcorn	甜玉米	Tián yùmǐ
Turnip	芜菁	Wú jīng
Zucchini	夏南瓜	Xià nánguā
Almond	杏仁	Xìngrén
Barley	大麦	Dàmài
Cashew	腰果	Yāoguǒ
Chickpea	鹰嘴豆	Yīng zuǐ dòu
Lentils	扁豆	Biǎndòu
Macadamia	澳洲坚果	Àozhōu jiānguǒ
Oats	燕麦	Yànmài
Peanut	花生	Huāshēng
Pecan	胡桃	Hútáo

Rice	米	Mǐ
Soy	**黄**豆	Huángdòu
Walnut	核桃	Hétáo
Wheat	小**麦**	Xiǎomài

Food and Drink

Barbeque	烧烤	Shāokǎo
Bread	面包	Miànbāo
Burgers	汉堡	Hànbǎo
Burrito	墨西哥卷饼	Mòxīgē juǎn bǐng
Cheese	起司	Qǐ sī
French fries	**薯**条	Shǔ tiáo
Egg fried rice	咖喱	Gālí

Eggs	蛋炒饭	Dàn chǎofàn
Fried chicken	蛋	Dàn
Fries	炸鸡	Zhá jī
Hotdogs	热狗	Règǒu
Pasta	意大利面条	Yìdàlì miàn tiáo
Pies	派	Pài
Pizza	比萨	Bǐsà
Salad	沙拉	Shālā
Salt	盐	Yán
Sandwich	三明治	Sānmíngzhì
Soup	汤	Tāng
Steak	牛扒	Niú bā
Stir-fry	热炒	Rè chǎo

Sushi	寿司	Shòusī
Taco	塔科	Tǎ kē
Tofu	豆腐	Dòufu
Butter	牛油	Niú yóu
Cake	蛋糕	Dàngāo
Chocolate	巧克力	Qiǎokèlì
Cookies	饼干	Bǐnggān
Crackers	苏打饼干	Sūdǎ bǐnggān
Dessert	甜点	Tiándiǎn
Doughnuts	甜甜圈	Tián tián quān
Ice cream	冰淇淋	Bīngqílín
Pancakes	薄煎饼	Báo jiānbing
Peanut butter	花生酱	Huāshēngjiàng

Scones	司康饼	Sī kāng bǐng
Sugar	糖	Táng
Sweets	糖果	Tángguǒ
Waffles	威化饼	Wēi huà bǐng
Yogurt	酸奶	Suānnǎi
Beer	啤酒	Píjiǔ
Cocktail	鸡尾酒	Jīwěijiǔ
Coffee	咖啡	Kāfēi
Hot chocolate	热可可	Rè kěkě
Juice	果汁	Guǒzhī
Milkshake	奶昔	Nǎi xī
Soda	苏打	Sūdǎ
Tea	茶	Chá

Water	水	Shuǐ
Wine	葡萄酒	Pútáojiǔ

In the House and Around Our Daily Lives

House	房屋	Fángwū
Garden	花园	Huāyuán
Gate	铁门	Tiě mén
Door	门	Mén
Front yard	前院	Qián yuàn
Pool	游泳池	Yóuyǒngchí
Window	窗口	Chuāngkǒu
Stairs	楼梯	Lóutī
Garage	车库	Chēkù

Corridor	走廊	Zǒuláng
Carpet	地毯	Dìtǎn
Floor	地板	Dìbǎn
Roof	屋顶	Wūdǐng
Walls	墙	Qiáng
Living room	客厅	Kètīng
Sofa	沙发	Shāfā
Remote controller	遥控器	Yáokòng qì
Television	电视	Diànshì
Bedroom	卧室	Wòshì
Bed	床	Chuáng
Pillow	枕头	Zhěntou
Curtain	窗帘	Chuānglián

Beddings	床上用品	Chuángshàng yòngpǐn
Wardrobe	衣柜	Yīguì
Clothes	衣服	Yīfú
Shirt	衬衫	Chènshān
Pants	裤子	Kùzi
Shoes	鞋子	Xiézi
Makeup	化妆品	Huàzhuāngpǐn
Kitchen	厨房	Chúfáng
Cupboard	橱柜	Chúguì
Chair	椅子	Yǐzi
Table	桌子	Zhuōzi
Fridge	冰箱	Bīngxiāng
Stove	炉子	Lúzǐ

Sink	水槽	Shuǐcáo
Bathroom	浴室	Yùshì
Shower	淋浴	Línyù
Bathtub	浴缸	Yùgāng
Tap	水龙头	Shuǐlóngtóu
Mirror	镜子	Jìngzi
Clock	时钟	Shízhōng
Decoration	装饰	Zhuāngshì
Painting	画作	Huàzuò
Lights	灯	Dēng
Car	汽车	Qìchē
Keys	钥匙	Yàoshi
Motorbike	摩托车	Mótuō chē

Bicycle	自行车	Zìxíngchē
Aeroplane	飞机	Fēijī
Bus	巴士站	Bāshì
Train	火车站	Huǒchē
Ship	船	Chuán
Laptop	笔记本电脑	Bǐjìběn diànnǎo
Computer	电脑	Diànnǎo
Smartphone	手机	Shǒujī
Telephone	电话	Diànhuà
Watch	手表	Shǒubiǎo

Society

School	学校	Xuéxiào
Hospital	医院	Yīyuàn
Police station	警察局	Jǐngchá jú
Fire brigade	消防队	Xiāofáng duì
Government	政府	Zhèngfǔ
Shopping mall	购物中心	Gòu wù zhòng xīn
Church	教会	Jiàohuì
University	大学	Dàxué
Park	公园	Gōngyuán
Neighbours	邻居	Línjū
Office	办公室	Bàngōngshì
Doctors	医生	Yīshēng

Nurses	护士	Hùshì
Police	警察	Jǐngchá
Firefighters	消防员	Xiāofáng yuán
Clerks	文员	Wényuán
Teachers	老师	Lǎoshī
Students	学生	Xuéshēng

Common Words

This	这个	Zhège
That	那个	Nàge
These	这些	Zhèxiē
Those	那些	Nàxiē
Good	好	Hǎo

Bad	坏	Huài
Morning	早上	Zǎoshàng
Afternoon	下午	Xiàwǔ
Evening	晚上	Wǎnshàng
Breakfast	早餐	Zǎocān
Lunch	午餐	Wǔcān
Supper	晚餐	Wǎncān
North	北	Běi
East	东	Dōng
South	南	Nán
West	西	Xī
Left	左	Zuǒ
Right	右	Yòu

Up	上	Shàng
Down	下	Xià
Centre	中央	Zhōngyāng
Outside	外	Wài
Inside	**内**	Nèi
High	高	Gāo
Low	低	Dī
Big	大	Dà
Small	小	Xiǎo

Conclusion

Having reached the end of this book, we want you to give yourself a pat on the back! You started your journey to learn Mandarin, and to have come this far is no small feat. At this point, you should be well acquainted with the historical significance of the Mandarin language, as well as be familiar with where it can be utilized both in your personal life and beyond. You will also have hopefully established a newfound yearning to continue learning Mandarin. Remember, your journey doesn't end here; this is only the beginning.

You have learned the basics of Mandarin, extending from the various types of tones to being able to differentiate between many different pinyin and Chinese characters. Now that you have successfully conquered this first book, you should be well apt to learn all of the Mandarin words within it, and you should also be able to start constructing some short and concise sentences.

Here are some ways you can progress from your current level:

- Start to studiously work through the workbook that comes with this book. Not only will it aid you in fine-tuning your character writing skills, but it will also show you where there are gaps in your knowledge, as well as which rules need to be revisited to fill these gaps. This book should act as your own personal encyclopedia for when you need to review some basic concepts.

- Why not try the HSK test? The HSK is a fantastic method for testing how well your reading, writing, listening, and speech have progressed. It will show you how well you are progressing and provide you with some context of what level of Mandarin you need to achieve to not only converse with native speakers, but also to be considered fluent.

- Start to follow the steps as mentioned in the previous chapters about fully integrating yourself within Mandarin. Start to change your technological devices to the Mandarin language. Also, try your best to find a native speaker with whom you can practice your speech and listening skills and who will correct you when you make a mistake. The only way that you will really progress is by challenging your current level of knowledge.

It is important to remember that you need to consistently be reviewing and learning new words. Repetition is key if your end goal is to master Mandarin. Make sure you are confident in your current abilities before you traverse into a new category of information. In this book, we purposefully did not focus too much on grammar, as you need to have a strong foundation in understanding the nuances of the language first. Your next focus will be to incorporate what you currently know into your everyday life.

You took the step that many others were too scared to take. You remained determined, dedicated, and realistic in your goal-setting in order to reach the end of this book. Remember that this book should be seen as a reference to you. Do not beat yourself up when you erroneously use a tone that was not there. Instead, revisit the content in this book so that you do not make the same mistake again.

You have come this far and will continue to venture even further. Well done, and good luck on the road ahead. Never forget that you are capable of more than you think you are. You will continue to grow from strength to strength on your journey in learning Mandarin.

References

AllSet Learning. (2020, May 3). *Four tones.* Chinese Pronunciation Wiki. https://resources.allsetlearning.com/chinese/pronunciation/Four_tones

Ben, E. (2018, March 15). *10 common mistakes language learners make (and how to fix them).* Matador Network. https://matadornetwork.com/read/10-common-mistakes-language-learners-make-fix/

Boogaard, K. (2019, January 25). *An explanation of SMART goals and how to write them.* Work Life by Atlassian. https://www.atlassian.com/blog/productivity/how-to-write-smart-goals#:~:text=SMART%20is%20an%20acronym%20that

China Highlights. (2019a). *Dragon Boat Festival 2019.* China Highlights. https://www.chinahighlights.com/festivals/dragon-boat-festival.htm

China Highlights. (2019b). *Qingming Festival.* China Highlights. https://www.chinahighlights.com/festivals/qingming-festival.htm

Free Language. (n.d.). *9 Steps to Overcome the Fear of Speaking a Foreign Language | Free Language.* Freelanguage.org. Retrieved December 19, 2020, from https://freelanguage.org/how-to-learn-languages/9-steps-to-overcome-the-fear-of-speaking-a-foreign-language

Global Exam Blog. (2016, September 7). *100 million students learning Mandarin in 2020.* GlobalExam Blog. https://global-exam.com/blog/en/100-million-students-learning-mandarin-in-

2020/#:~:text=The%20increase%20in%20students%20learnin
g

Huizhongmcmillen, A. (n.d.). *Easy as ABC: 8 Foolproof Tips for Learning
    Chinese Faster.* Retrieved December 17, 2020, from
    https://www.fluentu.com/blog/chinese/2016/01/18/tips-for-
    learning-chinese/

I Will Teach You A Language. (2017, July 10) . *7 Ways to Embrace
    Mistakes When Speaking a Foreign Language.* I Will Teach You A
    Language. https://iwillteachyoualanguage.com/blog/embrace-
    mistakes

McCollum-Martinez, C. (2019, January 10). *What Salary Will You Earn
    Teaching Abroad in China? | Go Overseas.* Www.Gooverseas.com.
    https://www.gooverseas.com/blog/teaching-english-in-china-
    salary

Minsky, C. (2016, September 12). *Five reasons why you should study in
    China.* Times Higher Education (THE).
    https://www.timeshighereducation.com/student/advice/five-
    reasons-why-you-should-study-china

Pinyin Guide. (n.d.). *Pinyin Guide | Pronunciation, FAQs and more.* Pinyin
    Guide. Retrieved December 16, 2020, from
    https://www.pinyin-guide.com/

Thought Co. (2019, June 15). *How Did Mandarin Become China's Official
    Language?*   ThoughtCo.
    https://www.thoughtco.com/introduction-to-mandarin-
    chinese-
    2278430#:~:text=Mandarin%20emerged%20as%20the%20lan
    guage

Wei, X. (2020, July 4). *Chinese productions attract global fanbase.* SHINE.
    https://www.shine.cn/feature/entertainment/2007041400/

World Data. (n.d.). *Chinese - Worldwide distribution.* Worlddata.Info. Retrieved December 17, 2020, from https://www.worlddata.info/languages/chinese.php

Yi, L. (2013). *Introduction to Chinese Characters | Year of China.* Www.Brown.Edu. https://www.brown.edu/about/administration/international-affairs/year-of-china/language-and-cultural-resources/introduction-chinese-characters/introduction-chinese-characters#:~:text=Oracle%20Bone%20Inscriptions%20refers%20to

All images were created using Krita software.

Learn Mandarin Chinese Workbook for Beginners

A Step-by-Step Textbook to Practice the Chinese Characters Quickly and Easily While Having Fun

Leo W. Chang

contained within this document, including, but not limited to, errors, omissions, or inaccuracies.

Table of Contents

Introduction

When learning a new language, emphasis is placed on practice. The more you practice, the faster you progress, and the better you get! This is exactly why this workbook has been included as a fundamental resource as you continue your journey in learning Mandarin. What you will find in this workbook is a more practical approach to learning the language. You will need to get your pencils sharpened as this is where you will be learning all about the different pinyin and their related Chinese characters.

There are three fundamental principles that are going to be focused on in this workbook. These are the domains of reading, writing, and translating. By now, you should have a good grasp of the different tones of pinyin, as well as how Chinese characters are written in terms of number of strokes, direction of strokes, as well as stroke order. These will be tested as you start to write out your first Chinese characters, along with their corresponding pinyin.

What is fantastic about learning pinyin is that you can type it on your phone's keyboard and, if set to Mandarin, it will even show you the corresponding Chinese character. This is a great way to continually interact with your Mandarin studies whilst going about your daily life.

This workbook is constructed in such a way that you are continually building on knowledge that has been previously obtained. We will be focusing on teaching you common dialogues between two people, how to read and write these dialogues in pinyin and Chinese characters, as well as adding a fun element by introducing some new words at the end of some chapters. You will be able to practice the dialogues and words by either writing them out in the spaces provided in this book or by writing them in a separate notebook. Remember, repetition is key, and it is the only proven method to help you learn and retain knowledge associated with studying Mandarin.

Do not feel the need to move quickly through this workbook. You should be working at a pace that is comfortable to you. We highly advise that you keep the first book close at hand as if you forget a tone or brushstroke rule, you will be able to quickly reference and revise the information. This is the exciting part of learning Mandarin, and our plan is to be with you throughout this journey, with each step that you take. Without further adieu, let's jump right in!

Chapter 1:

Greetings

One of the most common sets of phrases is "hello" and "thank you". Along with these are some common forms of initials and finals that should be constantly practiced. It is advised that you say these out loud in order to hear yourself and how you sound.

Hello

Context Specific Dialogues

Dialogue 1: Saying "Hello" to one other person.

Person A: Hello.

                   你好。

	Nǐ hǎo.
Person B:	Hello.
	你好。
	Nǐ hǎo.

Dialogue 2: Saying "Hello" to more than one person.

Person A:	Hello.
	你们好。
	Nǐ men hǎo.
Persons B and C:	Hello.
	你好。
	Nǐ hǎo.

Non-Context Specific Dialogue

Dialogue 3: Apologizing.

Person A:	I'm sorry!
	对不起!
	Duì bù qǐ!
Person B:	That's okay, it does not matter!
	没事，没关系!
	Méi shì, méi guān xì!

Initials and Finals

Initials and Finals that need to be studied:

Initials	Finals
b	i
p	u
m	ü
f	er
d	a
t	ia
n	ua
l	o
g	uo
k	e
h	ie
j	ue
q	ai
x	uai

	ei	
	uei (ui)	
		ao
		iao

Thank You

Context-Specific Dialogues

Dialogue 1: Saying "Thank you" to one other person.

Person A: Thank you!

                   谢谢你!

Xiè xiè nǐ!

Person B: Sure!

                        不客气!

                        Bù kè qì!

Dialogue 2: Saying "Thank you" to an elder (or a person that is older than you are).

Person A: Thank you!

                        谢谢您!

                        Xiè xiè nín!

Persons B and C: You are welcome!

                        不客气!

                        Bù kè qì!

Dialogue 3: Informally saying "Goodbye."

Person A: Goodbye!

                        再见!

                        Zài jiàn!

Person B: Bye!

                        再见!

                        Zài jiàn!

Initials and Finals

Initials and finals that need to be studied:

Initials	Finals
zh	ou
ch	iou (iu)
sh	an
r	ian
z	uan
c	üan
s	en
	in
	uen (un)
	ün
	ang
	iang
	uang
	eng

	ing	
	ueng	
		ong
	iong	

New Words and Phrases

It is important that you are always adding to your vocabulary each and every time you study Mandarin. In this section, we are going to give you some fun new words to try out, as well as their pinyin and Chinese characters so that you can start to recognize them in sentences and conversations. Don't forget to practice writing them in the spaces provided.

- One

  一

  _____

  Yī

- Two

  二

  _____

  Èr

  _____

- Three

_____

三

_____

Sān

_____

- Four

四

_____

Sì

_____

- Five

五

_____

Wǔ

_____

- Six

六

_____

Liù

_____

- Seven

七

_____

Qī

_____

- Eight

_____

八

_____

Bā

_____

- Nine

九

_____

Jiǔ

_____

- Ten

十

_____

Shí

_____

- Jacket

夹克

_____

Jiákè

_____

- Fish

鱼

_____

Yú

_____

- Ear

  耳

  _____

  Ěr

- Pen

  笔

  _____

  Bǐ

- Cat

  猫

  _____

  Māo

- Island

  岛

  _____

  Dǎo

- Flower

  花

  _____

Huā

- Chicken

鸡

Jī

- Shoes

鞋

Xié

- Summer

春

Chūn

- Spring

夏

Xià

- Autumn

秋

Qiū

- Winter

冬

Dōng

- Clock

时钟

Shí zhōng

- Hand

手

Shǒu

- Bear

熊

Xióng

- Clouds

  云

  _____

  Yún

  _____

- Stars

  星星

  _____

  Xīng xīng

  _____

- Friend

  朋友

  _____

  Péng yǒu

  _____

- Apple

  苹果

  _____

  Píng guǒ

  _____

- Bed

  床

  _____

  Chuáng_____

- Panda

  熊猫
  _____

  Xióng māo
  _____

- Watch

  手表
  _____

  Shǒu biǎo
  _____

- Ball

  球
  _____

  Qiú
  _____

- Egg

  蛋
  _____

  Dàn
  _____

- Hamburger

  汉堡包_____

  Hàn bǎo bāo _____

- McDonalds

  麦当劳_____

  Mài dāng láo _____
- Adidas

  阿迪达斯 _____

  Ā dí dá sī_____
- Nike

  耐克 _____

  Nài kè _____
- David Beckham

  大卫贝克汉姆

  _____

  Dà wèi bèi kè hàn mǔ

  _____
- Harry Potter

  哈利 波特

  _____

  Hā lì bō tè

  _____
- Class begins.

上课

Shàng kè

● Class is over.

下课

Xià kè

● Look at this.

看这个

Kànzhège

● Read after me.

随我念

Suí wǒ niàn

● Read together.

一起念

Yī qǐ niàn

- Any questions?

  有问题吗

  Yǒu wèn tí ma?

Chapter 2:

Formalities

It is customary to ask individuals a few questions when you first meet them. As someone who is still at the beginning phases of learning Mandarin, it is vital that you ask these questions at all encounters, not only so that you become comfortable with asking them, but also to hone your skills. These questions can feel rather intimidating the first time that they are asked, but they will become second -nature as soon as you start to interact with a wider variety of those who speak Mandarin.

Use what you have learned in the previous chapter to start stringing together the beginning of a conversation as you would typically do in English.

Names

Context Specific Dialogue

Dialogue 1: Asking someone for their name.

Person A:	What is your name?
	你的名字叫什么？
	Nǐ de míng zì jiào shén me?
Person B:	My name is Xiao Ming.
	我的名字叫小明。
	Wǒ de míng zì jiào Xiao Míng.

Non-Context Specific Dialogues

Dialogue 2: Asking whether someone is a teacher or not.

Person A: Are you a teacher?

                   你是老师吗?

                   Nǐ shì lǎo shī ma?

Person B: No, I am not. I am a student.

                   不，我不是. 我是学生。

                   Bù, wǒ bù shì, wǒ shì xué shēng.

Dialogue 3: Enquiring whether someone is Chinese.

Person A: Are you Chinese?

                   你是中国人吗?

                   Nǐ shì Zhōng Guó rén ma?

Person B: No, I am not. I am French.

                   不，我不是，我是法国人。

                   Bù, wǒ bù shì, wǒ shì Fà guó rén.

Practice Dialogues

It is important to avoid only translating from English to Mandarin. By doing this, you are teaching yourself to think in one direction, which will hinder the speed at which you make progress. What we want you to do here is to read the pinyin, and then write down what you think the Chinese characters are based on the pinyin, as well as the English translation. Once you have completed this, check your answers and refine your translations. You can then go ahead and answer the question in pinyin and Chinese characters to ensure you understand everything that has been taught thus far.

Dialogue 1:

Nǐ jiào shén me míng zi?

你叫什么名字?

What is your name?

Answer:

_____
_____
_____
_____
_____

Dialogue 2:

Nǐ shì Zhōng Guó rén ma?

你是中国人吗?

Are you Chinese?

Answer:

_____
_____
_____
_____

Dialogue 3:

Nǐ shì Měi guó rén ma?

你是美国人吗？

Are you American?

Answer:

_____

_____

_____

_____

Dialogue 4:

Nǐ shì lǎo shī ma?

你是老师吗？

Are you a teacher?

Answer:

_____

_____

_____

_____

Dialogue 5:

Nǐ shì xué sheng ma?

你是学生吗?

Are you a student?

Answer:

_____

_____

_____

_____

_____

_____

Initials and Finals

Identify the initials and finals in the following words. Practice them by enunciating their tones correctly. You will also see their English translation, as well as their Chinese characters next to the pinyin.

Pinyin	Chinese character(s)	English
Xiū xi	休息	Rest
Xīng qī	星期	Week
Jī jí	积极	Positive
Jī qì	机器	Machine
Xiāng jiāo	香蕉	Banana
Xìng qù	兴趣	Interests

Xiǎo qū	小区	Community
Jì xù	继续	Carry on
Xǐ zǎo	洗澡	To shower/bathe
Dǎ sǎo	打扫	Clean up
Zuó tiān	昨天	Yesterday
Zǎo shang	早上	Morning
Sān cì	三次	Three times
Cāo chǎng	操场	Playground
Zì jǐ	自己	Self
Hán zì	汉字	Chinese characters

Mandarin Teacher

Context Specific Dialogue

Dialogue 1: Asking whether an individual is your Mandarin teacher.

Person A: Who is she?

她是谁?

Tā shì shéi?

Person B: She is my Mandarin teacher. Her name is Mei Yong.

她是我的中文老师。她的名字叫美咏。

Tā shì wǒ de zhōng wén lǎo shī. Tā de míng zì jiào Mei Yong.

Non-Context Specific Dialogues

Dialogue 2: Asking about where someone comes from.

Person A:	Which country are you from?
	你来自哪个国家?
	Nǐ lái zì nǎ ge guó jiā?
Person B:	The United States of America. What about you?
	美国。你呢?
	Měi Guó. Nǐ ne?
Person A:	I am from China.
	我来自中国。
	Wǒ lái zì Zhōng Guó.

Dialogue 3: Asking the relationship of one person to another.

Person A:	Who is he?
	他是谁?
	Tā shì shéi?
Person B:	He is my classmate.
	他是我同学。
	Tā shì wǒ tóng xué.

Person A:	What about her? Is she your classmate?
	那**她**呢? **她**是**你**同学吗?
	Nà tā ne? Tā shì nǐ tóng xué ma?
Person B:	No, she is not. She is my friend.
	不, **她**不是。 **她**是我朋友。Bù,
	tā bù shì. Tā shì wǒ péng yǒu.

Practice Dialogues

Complete and answer the following questions which are in pinyin. If you get stuck, refer back to the notes and previous chapters in order to solidify your knowledge.

Dialogue 1:

Nǐ shì nǎ guó rén?

你是**哪**国人?

Which country are you from?

Answer:

_____
_____
_____
_____
_____
_____

Dialogue 2:

Nǐ jiào shén me míng zi?

你叫什么名字?

What is your name?

Answer:

_____

_____

_____

_____

_____

Dialogue 3:

Nǐ de Hàn yǔ lǎo shī shì nǎ guó rén?

你的汉语老师是哪国人?

Which country is your Mandarin teacher from?

Answer:

_____

_____

_____

_____

_____

Dialogue 4:

Nǐ de Hàn yǔ lǎo shī jiào shén me míng zi?

你的汉语老师叫什么名字?

What is the name of your Mandarin teacher?

Answer:

_____

_____

_____

_____

_____

_____

_____

Dialogue 5:

Nǐ de Zhōng Guó péng you shì shéi?

你的中国朋友是谁?

Who is your Chinese friend?

Answer:
_____

_____

_____

_____

_____

Initials and Finals

Identify the initials and finals in the following words. Practice them by enunciating their tones correctly. You will also see their English translation as well as their Chinese characters next to the pinyin.

Pinyin	Chinese character(s)	English
Zhī shì	知识	Knowledge
Rèn shì	认识	Recognize

Rán shāo	燃烧	Burn
Shǒu shù	手术	Surgery
Chú shī	厨师	Chef
Cháng shì	常识	General knowledge
Rè nào	热闹	Lively
Shāng chǎng	商场	Mall
Shēng rì	生日	Birthday
Shì shí	事实	Truth
Chū chāi	出差	Business trip
Chāo shì	超市	Supermarket
Shàng Chē	上车	Enter the car
Chāo rén	超人	Superman
Cháng chéng	长城	The Great Wall of China
Chōng zhí	充值	Recharge

Family, Age and Complex Numbers

Context Specific Dialogues

Dialogue 1: Asking the amount of people in another's family.

Person A:	How many people are there in your family?
	你家有几口人?
	Nǐ jiā yǒu jǐ kǒu rén?
Person B:	There are four.
	我有四个。
	Wǒ yǒu sì gè.

Dialogue 2: Asking how old one's daughter is.

Person A:	How old is your daughter?
	你女儿多大了?
	Nǐ nǚ ér duō dà le?
Person B:	She is four years old.
	她四岁了。
	Tā sì suì le.

Non-Context Specific Dialogue

Dialogue 3: Asking about the relatives of another person.

Person A:	How old is Professor Li?
	李教授几岁了？
	Lǐ jiào shòu jǐ suì le?
Person B:	She is 50 years old.
	她五十岁了。
	Tā wǔ shí suì le.
Person A:	What about her daughter?
	那她女儿呢？
	Nà tā nǚ ér ne?
Person B:	Her daughter is 20.
	她二十岁了。
	Tā èr shí suì le.

Practice Dialogues

These practice dialogues will test your ability to have solidified your current knowledge. If you get stuck, feel free to revisit the previous chapters. Make sure that all the information and knowledge in these first two chapters are fully understood, as they will be teased out in more detail as the book progresses.

Dialogue 1:

Nǐ jiā yǒu jǐ kǒu rén?

你家有几口人?

How many people are there in your family?

Answer:

_____

_____

_____

_____

_____

_____

Dialogue 2:

Nǐ jīn nián duō dà le?

你今年多大了?

How old are you this year?

Answer:

_____

_____

_____

_____

_____

Dialogue 3:

Nǐ de Hàn yǔ lǎo shī jīn nián duō dà le?

你的汉语老师今年几岁了?

How old is your Mandarin teacher this year?

Answer:

_____
_____
_____
_____
_____
_____

Dialogue 4:

Nǐ de Zhōng Guó péng you jiā yǒu jǐ kǒu rén?

你的中国朋友家有几口人？

How many people are there in your Chinese friend's family?

Answer:

_____
_____
_____
_____
_____
_____

Dialogue 5:

Nǐ de Zhōng Guó péng you jīn nián duō dà le ?

你的中国朋友今年多大了？

How old is your Chinese friend this year?

Answer:

_____
_____
_____
_____

Age and Numbers

Learning how to count from one to ten creates a very good foundation when learning the intricacies of numbers in Mandarin. However, when asking and receiving questions regarding age, it is important to understand how the numbers that express an age are derived in Mandarin.

The table below will give you a very simple approach to constructing the different numbers in pinyin. It uses two main axes with one through ten being on the horizontal axis and factors of ten on the vertical axis. Following these axes to a specific number in the table will allow you to visually see how a specific number is pronounced, as well as how the pinyin was constructed. Take a look below:

	1 yī	2 èr	3 sān	4 sì	5 wǔ	6 liù	7 qī	8 bā	9 jiǔ
10 shí	11 shí yī	12 shí èr	13 shí sān	14 shí sì	15 shí wǔ	16 shí liù	17 shí qī	18 shí bā	19 shí jiǔ
20 èr shí	21 èr shí yī	22 èr shí èr	23 èr shí sān	24 èr shí sì	25 èr shí wǔ	26 èr shí liù	27 èr shí qī	28 èr shí bā	29 èr shí jiǔ
30 sān shí	31 sān shí yī	32 sān shí èr	33 sān shí sān	34 sān shí sì	35 sān shí wǔ	36 sān shí liù	37 sān shí qī	38 sān shí bā	39 sān shí jiǔ
40 sì shí	41 sì shí yī	42 sì shí èr	43 sì shí sān	44 sì shí sì	45 sì shí wǔ	46 sì shí liù	47 sì shí qī	48 sì shí bā	49 sì shí jiǔ
50 wǔ shí	51 wǔ shí yī	52 wǔ shí èr	53 wǔ shí sān	54 wǔ shí sì	55 wǔ shí wǔ	56 wǔ shí liù	57 wǔ shí qī	58 wǔ shí bā	59 wǔ shí jiǔ
60 liù shí	61 liù shí yī	62 liù shí èr	63 liù shí sān	64 liù shí sì	65 liù shí wǔ	66 liù shí liù	67 liù shí qī	68 liù shí bā	69 liù shí jiǔ
70 qī shí	71 qī shí yī	72 qī shí èr	73 qī shí sān	74 qī shí sì	75 qī shí wǔ	76 qī shí liù	77 qī shí qī	78 qī shí bā	79 qī shí jiǔ
80 bā shí	81 bā shí yī	82 bā shí èr	83 bā shí sān	84 bā shí sì	85 bā shí wǔ	86 bā shí liù	87 bā shí qī	88 bā shí bā	89 bā shí jiǔ

90 jiǔ shí	91 jiǔ shí yī	92 jiǔ shí èr	93 jiǔ shí sān	94 jiǔ shí sì	95 jiǔ shí wǔ	96 jiǔ shí liù	97 jiǔ shí qī	98 jiǔ shí bā	99 jiǔ shí jiǔ

Now that you have the different pinyin translations for the English numbers, it is time to correlate them to translated Chinese characters. Using the amount of Chinese characters associated with each number below, try to divide the above pinyin into segments that represent the number in question. This will allow you to train your eye in being able to recognize and read syllables. The Chinese character translations for the above pinyin are as follows:

	1 一	2 二	3 三	4 四	5 五	6 六	7 七	8 八	9 九
10 十	11 十一	12 十二	13 十三	14 十四	15 十五	16 十六	17 十七	18 十八	19 十九
20 二十	21 二十一	22 二十二	23 二十三	24 二十四	25 二十五	26 二十六	27 二十七	28 二十八	29 二十九
30 三十	31 三十一	32 三十二	33 三十三	34 三十四	35 三十五	36 三十六	37 三十七	38 三十八	39 三十九
40 四十	41 四十一	42 四十二	43 四十三	44 四十四	45 四十五	46 四十六	47 四十七	48 四十八	49 四十九

50 五十	51 五十一	52 五十二	53 五十三	54 五十四	55 五十五	56 五十六	57 五十七	58 五十八	59 五十九
60 六十	61 六十一	62 六十二	63 六十三	64 六十四	65 六十五	66 六十六	67 六十七	68 六十八	69 六十九
70 七十	71 七十一	72 七十二	73 七十三	74 七十四	75 七十五	76 七十六	77 七十七	78 七十八	79 七十九
80 八十	81 八十一	82 八十二	83 八十三	84 八十四	85 八十五	86 八十六	87 八十七	88 八十八	89 八十九
90 九十	91 九十一	92 九十二	93 九十三	94 九十四	95 九十五	96 九十六	97 九十七	98 九十八	99 九十九

Now that you have all the necessary translations of the different numbers, try creating your own dialogues. These dialogues can include asking others which number comes after another or enquiring as to the age of another person. The more creative you become, the more fun you will have, and the more fun you have, the better your memory will be of specific information, knowledge, and concepts. With that being said, we have reached the part in the chapter where we give you some new and fun words to learn.

New Words and Phrases

- One hundred

  一百

  _____

  Yī bǎi

  _____

- Zero

  零

  _____

  Líng

  _____

- Sing

  唱

  _____

  Chàng

  _____

- Remember

  记得

  _____

  Jì dé

  _____

- Introduce

介绍

Jiè shào

- Explain

说明

Shuō míng

- Climb

爬

Pá

- Believe

相信

Xiāng xìn

- Child

孩子

Há izi

- Older brother

哥哥

___

Gē gē

- Younger brother

弟弟

___

Dì dì

- Older sister

姊姊

___

Jiě jie

- Younger sister

妹妹

___

Mèi mei

- Son

儿子

___

Ér zi

- Daughter

女儿

Nǚ ér

- Accept

接受

Jiē shòu

- Borrow

借

Jiè

- Change

更改

Gēng gǎi

- Complete

完成

_____

Wán chéng

_____

- Hide

躲

_____

Duǒ

_____

- Give

给

_____

Gěi

_____

- Meet

遇到

_____

Yù dào _____

- Need

需要

_____

Xū yào _____

- Open

打开

Dǎ kāi

- Look

看

Kàn

- Speak

说话

Shuō huà

- Stand

站

Zhàn

- Study

读书

Dú shū
- Butterfly

蝴蝶

Hú dié

- Eagle

老鹰

Lǎo yīng

- Roots

树根

Shù gēn

- Lavender

薰衣草

Xūn yī cǎo

- Ocean

海洋

Hǎi yáng

- Waves

  波浪

  _____

  Bō làng _____

- Beach

  海滩

  _____

  Hǎi tān _____

- Beetroot

  红菜头

  _____

  Hóng cài tóu
  _____

- Bell pepper

  灯笼椒

  _____

  Dēng lóng jiāo _____

- Pasta

  意大利面条

  _____

  Yì dà lì miàn tiáo
  _____

- Doughnuts

  甜甜圈

  _____

  Tián tián quān _____

- How have you been?

  你最近好吗？

  _____

  Nǐ zuì jìn hǎo ma?

  _____

- Good morning

  早安

  _____

  Zǎo ān

  _____

- Good afternoon

  午安

  _____

  Wǔ ān

  _____

- Good evening/good night

  晚安

  _____

Wǎ nān

_____

- Pleased to meet you

高兴认识你

_____

Gāo xìng rèn shí nǐ

_____

- Let us meet soon

我们再约

_____

Wǒ men zài yuē

_____

Chapter 3:

Daily Living

The foundation that you have now built contains information and knowledge that will allow you to survive in a Mandarin-speaking country. However, you do not want to just survive, but thrive. Thus, we will now add some meat to the bones, ensuring that your conversations have substance and that interactions with those who are fluent in Mandarin do not become awkward. The topics may seem rather random in terms of content; however, these are the most common categories of information that should be obtained.

Dates

You want to make sure that you know the months and days of the week. You may find yourself in a situation where someone asks you what day it is, and because you are kind and courteous, you will most likely want to help. That is also a value ingrained within Chinese culture—assisting where you can. With that said, let's dive right in!

Context Specific Dialogues

Dialogue 1: Asking someone what the date and day of the week is.

Person A: Excuse me, what is the date today?

对不起，请问今天几号？

Duì bùqǐ, qǐngwèn jīn tiān jǐ hào?

Person B: It is December 12th.

十二月十二日。

Shí èr yuè shí èr rì.

Person A: What day is it today?

今天星期几?

Jīn tiān xīng qí jǐ?

Person B: It is Friday.

星期五。

Xīng qí wǔ.

Dialogue 2: Asking the date and day of the week using past and future tenses.

Person A: What was the date yesterday?

昨天是几号?

Zuó tiān shì jǐ hào?

Person B: It was Monday, July 17th.

星期一, 七月十七日。

Xīng qí yī, qī yuè shí qī rì.

Person A: What about tomorrow?

那明天呢?

Nà míng tiān ne?

Person B: It is Wednesday, July 19th.

星期三，七月十九日。

Xīng qí sān, qī yuè shí jiǔ rì.

Non-Context Specific Dialogue

Dialogue 3: Asking whether someone will be going to school.

Person A: Tomorrow is Saturday. Will you go to school?

明天是星期六。 你会去学校吗?

Míng tiān shì xīng qí liù. Nǐ huì qù xué xiào ma?

Person B: Yes, I will.

是，我会去。

Shì, wǒ huì qù.

Person A: What are you going to do there?

你会在那里做什么?

Nǐ huì zài nà lǐ zuò shén me?

Person B: I am going there to do some reading.

我要去看书。

Wǒ yào qù kàn shū.

Practice Dialogues

Months and days of the week are easy to understand, but they just need to have their components well understood. Before we jump into the practice dialogues, let's go through what the months and days of the week are when translated into pinyin and their Chinese characters. The months of the year are as follows:

English	Pinyin	Chinese characters
January	yī yuè	一月
February	èr yuè	二月
March	sān yuè	三月
April	sì yuè	四月
May	wǔ yuè	五月
June	liù yuè	六月
July	qī yuè	七月
August	bā yuè	八月
September	jiǔ yuè	九月
October	shí yuè	十月
November	shí yī yuè	十一月

December	shí èr yuè	十二月

As you can see above, there is a very distinct pattern that can be used in order to correctly identify and record the months of the year. The numbers from one to ten have their pinyin included in the respective month from one to ten. As soon as the tenth month is reached (October), the names of 11 and 12 are used. At the end, the word 'yuè' is added to show reference to the name of a month.

We will now delve into the different days of the week. These are as follows:

English	Pinyin	Chinese characters
Monday	xīng qī yī	星期一
Tuesday	xīng qī èr	星期二
Wednesday	xīng qī sān	星期三
Thursday	xīng qī sì	星期四
Friday	xīng qī wǔ	星期五
Saturday	xīng qī liù	星期六
Sunday	xīng qī tiān / xīng qī rì	星期天 / 星期日

The naming of the days of the week follow a similar pattern to that of the months of the year. However, the exception is with Sunday. The words 'xīng qī' are used to refer to a day of the week. However, the number seven is also 'qī'. Thus, to avoid confusion, the seventh day of the week (Sunday) has slightly different pinyin and Chinese characters.

Now that we have established a good base in terms of dates, months, and days of the week, we can now move on to the practice dialogues.

Dialogue 1:

Jīn tiān jǐ yuè jǐ hào xīng qī jǐ?

今天几月几号星期几?

What is today's month, date, and day?

Answer:

_____
_____
_____
_____
_____
_____

Dialogue 2:

Míng tiān jǐ yuè jǐ hào xīng qī jǐ?

明天几月几号星期几?

What is tomorrow's month, date, and day?

Answer:

_____
_____
_____
_____
_____

Dialogue 3:

Zuó tiān jǐ yuè jǐ hào xīng qī jǐ?

昨天几月几号星期几?

What is yesterday's month, date, and day?

Answer:

_____

_____

_____

_____

_____

_____

Dialogue 4:

Míng tiān nǐ qù nǎr zuò shén me?

明天你去哪做什么?

Where are you going tomorrow, and what will you be doing?

Answer:

_____

_____

_____

_____

_____

Dialogue 5:

Xīng qīrì nǐ qù nǎr zuò shén me ?

星期日你去哪做什么?

Where are you going, and what will you be doing on Sunday?

Answer:

_____

_____

_____

_____

_____

_____

Initials and Finals

Identify the initials and finals in the following words. Practice them by enunciating their tones correctly. You will also see their English translation and Chinese characters next to the pinyin.

Pinyin	Chinese character(s)	English
Guó jiā	国家	Country
Zuó tiān	昨天	Yesterday
Míng tiān	明天	Tomorrow
Nián qīng	年轻	Young
Lóu fáng	楼房	Building
Lán qiú	篮球	Basketball
Míng nián	明年	Next year
Píng guǒ	苹果	Apple

Pí jiǔ	**啤**酒	Beer
Niú nǎi	牛奶	Milk
Yóu yǒng	游泳	Swim
Huán jìng	环境	Environment
Hán jià	寒假	Winter holiday
Niú ròu	牛肉	Steak
Yóu xì	游戏	Game

Ordering Food and Drink

You will find yourself more times than you might think ordering food and drink from either a restaurant or a night market. The latter is extremely common in native Mandarin-speaking countries. So, to be able to communicate effectively, we thought it would be apt to focus on learning some new terms, whilst revising what was learned in the previous book.

Context Specific Dialogues

Dialogue 1: Ordering something to drink and eat at a restaurant.

Person A: What would you like to drink?

               你要喝什么？

               Nǐ yào hē shén me?

Person B: I'd like some tea.

               我想喝茶。

Wǒ xiǎng hē chá.

Person A: What would you like to eat?

你要吃什么？

Nǐ yào chī shén me?

Person B: I would like some rice please.

我想吃饭。

Wǒ xiǎng chī fàn.

Non-Context Specific Dialogue

Dialogue 2: Answering a question about what you want to buy at a store.

Person A: What would you like to do this afternoon?

你今天下午想做什么？

Nǐ jīn tiān xià wǔ xiǎng zuò shén me?

Person B: I would like to go shopping.

我想去逛街。

Wǒ xiǎng qù guàng jiē.

Person A: What do you want to buy?

你想买什么？

Nǐ xiǎng mǎi shén me?

Person B:	I want to buy a cup.
	我想买杯子。
	Wǒ xiǎng mǎi bēi zi.

Dialogue 3: Asking about the price of items.

Person A:	Hello! How much is this cup?
	你好！这杯子多少钱？
	Nǐ hǎo, zhè bēi zi duō shǎo qián?
Person B:	28 yuan.
	二十八元。
	Èr shí bā yuán.
Person A:	What about that one?
	那这个呢？
	Nà zhè ge ne?
Person B:	That one is 18 yuan.
	那个十八元。
	Nà gè shí bā yuán.

Amounts of Money

As with all other countries, Mandarin-speaking countries will use a specific currency. However, it may happen that a specific country may not use the 'yuan' (元) as their currency. It is therefore recommended to do some research regarding the most common currencies that are used in the country that you are planning to visit/emigrate to.

The reason that it is important to learn both the pinyin and Chinese characters for specific values is that a price will not necessarily always have numerical values for you to identify. You may find that the price will be written purely in Chinese characters. To curb any undue anxiety and confusion, here are a few values to note:

English	Pinyin	Chinese characters
One yuan	yī yuan	一元
Five yuan	wǔ yuan	五元
Ten yuan	shí yuan	十元
50 yuan	wǔshí	五十元
100 yuan	yī bǎi yuan	一百元

Practice Dialogues

You are getting closer and closer to being able to operate effectively on your own in any native Mandarin -speaking country. So, to make sure you are up to scratch, why don't you answer the following dialogues based on the questions written in pinyin? We challenge you to write your answer in English, pinyin, and Chinese characters. The practice dialogues that have been prepared for you are as follows:

Dialogue 1:

Nǐ xiǎng chī shén me?

你想吃什么?

What would you like to eat?

Answer:

_____
_____
_____
_____
_____
_____

Dialogue 2:

Nǐ xiǎng hē shén me?

你想喝什么?

What would you like to drink?

Answer:

_____
_____
_____
_____

Dialogue 3:

Míng tiān xià wǔ nǐ xiǎng zuò shén me?

明天下午你想做什么?

What would you like to do tomorrow afternoon?

Answer:

_____

_____

_____

_____

Dialogue 4:

Nǐ qù nǎge shāng diàn mǎi bēi zi?

你去哪个商店买杯子?

You went to that shop to buy a cup?

Answer:

_____

_____

_____

_____

Dialogue 5:

Yí ge bēi zi duō shao qián?

一个杯子多少钱?

How much is a cup?

Answer:

_____
_____
_____
_____
_____
_____

Initials and Finals

Pinyin	Chinese character(s)	English
Lǎo shī	老师	Teacher
Měi tiān	每天	Every day
Hǎ ibiān	海边	Beach
Yǐ jīng	已经	Already
Lǎo rén	老人	Old person
Měi nián	每年	Every year
Hǎi mián	海绵	Sponge
Yǐ qián	以前	Before

Yǔ sǎn	雨伞	Umbrella
Měi hǎo	美好	Beautiful
Xǐ zǎo	洗澡	Shower/bath
Biǎo yǎn	表演	Perform/performance
Yǒu yòng	有用	Useful
Měi lì	美丽	Beautiful
Gǎn xiè	感谢	Gratitude
Biǎo xiàn	表现	Performance

Occupations

One of the typical points of conversation is to ask someone what their occupation is. Not only does this open up the conversation into an array of different avenues in terms of follow-up questions, but it also acts as a filler question when you feel that there is an awkward silence ensuing. Asking about another's occupation can be seen as quite a personal question, so it is important to start off with the appropriate greetings before jumping into more person-specific questions. For now, focus on obtaining the correct pinyin and Chinese character translations.

Context Specific Dialogues

Dialogue 1: Asking where someone works.

Person A: Where do you work?

                      你在哪里工作?

                      Nǐ zài nǎlǐ gōng zuò?

Person B: I work in a school.

我在学校工作。

Wǒ zài xué xiào gōng zuò.

Person A: Where does your son work?

你儿子在哪工作？

Nǐ ér zi zài nǎ gōng zuò.

Person B: My son works in a hospital. He is a doctor.

他在医院工作。他是医生。

Tā zài yī yuàn gōng zuò. Tā shì yī shēng.

Non-Context Specific Dialogue

Dialogue 2: Asking where somebody's family member is.

Person A: Is your father at home?

你父亲在家吗？

Nǐ fù qīn zài jiā ma?

Person B: No, he is not.

不，他不在。

Bù, tā bù zài.

Person A: Where is he?

他在哪？

Tā zài nǎ?

Person B:	He is in the hospital.
	他在医院。
	Tā zài yī yuàn.

Dialogue 3: Asking the whereabouts of one's animals.

Person A:	Where is the kitty?
	猫咪在哪?
	Māo mī zài nǎ?
Person B:	The kitty is over there.
	猫咪在那。
	Māo mī zài nà.
Person A:	Where is the puppy?
	小狗在哪?
	Xiǎo gǒu zài nǎ?
Person B:	The puppy is under the chair.
	小狗在椅子底下。
	Xiǎo gǒu zài yǐ zi dǐ xia.

Based on the non- context specific dialogues, one is able to see how there is a common manner in which we refer to people and animals. The questions remain specific and build on the information and knowledge that you have already obtained in previous chapters. If you find yourself struggling, we encourage you to revisit and revise the previously learned content. Remember that it is okay to forget; relearning concepts makes you a better student!

Focusing on the context specific dialogue, it is important that we delve a bit deeper into the various types of occupations that exist. Below, you will find a few examples of different occupations, their pinyin, and their corresponding Chinese characters:

English	Pinyin	Chinese characters
Engineer	Gōng chéng shī	工程师
Shopkeeper	Diàn zhǔ	店主
Banker	Yín háng jiā	银行家
Policeman	Jǐng chá	警察
Pilot	Fēi xíng yuán	飞行员
Lawyer	Lǜ shī	律师
Teacher	Lǎo shī	老师
Professor	Jiào shòu	教授
Scientist	Kē xué jiā	科学家
Pharmacist	Yào jì shī	药剂师
Athlete	Yùn dòng yuán	运动员
Dentist	Yá yī	牙医

Accountant	Kuài jì	会计
Driver	Sī jī	司机

Practice Dialogues

These dialogues combine all the context specific and non-context specific dialogues that have been learned thus far. It is a fantastic way to gauge the progress that you have made. At this point in the workbook, it is highly advised that you implement "revision days" into your study timetable. Depending on the pace at which you are studying, more than one revision day may be necessary in order to concretize the information. Examples of dialogues that are related to the 'Occupation' subheading, are as follows:

Dialogue 1:

Xiǎo gǒu zài nǎr?

小狗在**哪**?

Where is the puppy?

Answer:

_____
_____
_____
_____
_____
_____

Dialogue 2:

Tā zài nǎr gōng zuò?

他在**哪**工作?

Where is he working?

Answer:

_____

_____

_____

_____

_____

_____

Dialogue 3:

Tā ér zi zài nǎr gōng zuò?

他儿子在哪工作?

Where is his son working?

Answer:

_____

_____

_____

_____

_____

_____

Dialogue 4:

Tā bà ba zài jiā ma?

她爸爸在家吗?

Is her dad at home?

Answer:

_____

_____

_____

_____

Dialogue 5:

Tā bà ba zài nǎr ne?

她爸爸在哪呢？

Where is her dad?

Answer:

Initials and Finals

Pinyin	Chinese character(s)	English
Xià tiān	夏天	Summer
Diàn dēng	电灯	Electric light
Chàng gē	唱歌	Sing
Jiàn kāng	健康	Healthy
Qù nián	去年	Last year
Diàn chí	电池	Battery
Fù xí	复习	Revise
Dì tú	地图	Map
Tiào wǔ	跳舞	Dance
Diàn yǐng	电影	Movie
Hàn yǔ	汉语	Mandarin Chinese
Dì tiě	地铁	Subway

Shuì jiào	睡觉	Sleep
Diàn shì	电视	Television
Hàn zì	汉字	Chinese characters
Jiàn miàn	见面	Meet

Actions and Questions

When wanting to ask for assistance, or to use a chair that is at someone's table, it is important that the correct vocabulary is used. Not only should the request resemble a question to prompt an answer, but the question needs to be well understood so that the other person can give an accurate answer. It is human nature to be inquisitive, which means that you may find yourself asking questions to someone about someone else. This can be a fantastic way to strategize for a conversation that you may want to have with that person.

Whether it be asking to sit in a communal area or inquiring as to what objects are present on different surfaces, we will be covering many different actions and questions that are commonly utilized during one's daily life.

Context Specific Dialogues

Dialogue 1: Asking whether a seat is taken.

Person A: Is this seat taken?

这座位有人坐了吗?

Zhè zuò wèi yǒu rén zuò le ma?

Person B: No it is not.

不，没有。

Bù, méi yǒu.

Person A: Can I sit here?

我可以坐着吗?

Wǒ kě yǐ zuò zhe ma?

Person B: Yes, please.

可以，请。

Kě yǐ, qǐng.

Dialogue 2: Asking information about others.

Person A: Who is the person in the front?

前头那个人是谁?

Qián tou nà gè rén shì shéi?

Person B: She is Wang Yang. She works in a hospital.

她是王梅。她在医院工作。

Tā shì wáng méi. Tā zài yī yuàn gōng zuò.

Person A: What about the person at the back? What is his name?

那后头那个人呢？他叫什么名字？

Nà hòu tou nà gè rén ne? Tā jiào shén me míng zì?

Person B:　　　　　　He is Xie Zhang. He works in a store.

他叫谢长。他在店里工作。

Tā jiào xiè zhǎng. Tā zài diàn lǐ gōng zuò.

Dialogue 3: Asking about where an object is.

Person A:　　　　　　What is there on that desk?

桌上有什么？

Zhuō shàng yǒu shén me?

Person B:　　　　　　There is a computer and a book.

有一台电脑和一本书。

Yǒu yī tái diàn nǎo hé yī běn shū.

Person A:　　　　　　Where is the cup?

杯子在哪？

Bēi zi zài nǎ?

Person B:　　　　　　It is in the drawer of the desk.

在**桌**子的抽屉里。

Zài zhuō zi de chōu tì lǐ.

Practice Dialogues

The objects that are present in these dialogues can be substituted with other everyday objects. The sentence will still make sense after the object swap has occurred. For example, if one were to say, "Where is the cup?" and were to substitute "cup" with "knife" by simply using the Chinese character for "knife" with that of the one for "cup", the sentence would be complete and perfectly understood by anyone who has studied Mandarin.

Let's try some practice dialogues to delve deeper into possible sentence structures. The examples are as follows:

Dialogue 1:

Diàn nǎo zài nǎr?

电脑在**哪**?

Where is the computer?

Answer:

_____

_____

_____

_____

_____

_____

Dialogue 2:

Shū zài nǎr?

书在哪?

Where is the book?

Answer:

_____

_____

_____

_____

_____

_____

Dialogue 3:

Zhuō zi lǐmiàn yǒu shén me?

桌子里面有什么?

What is inside the table?

Answer:

_____

_____

_____

_____

_____

_____

Dialogue 4:

Nǎ ge rén shì Wáng Fāng?

那个人是王芳吗?

Is that person Wang Fang?

Answer:

_____

_____

_____

_____

_____

_____

Dialogue 5:

Nǎ ge rén shì Xiè Péng?

那个人是谢鹏?

Is that person Xie Peng?

Answer:

_____

_____

_____

_____

_____

_____

Initials and Finals

The initials and finals, which you should be able to identify below, act as an extensive list of common terms of reference to other people and objects. Thus, it is important for you to spend sufficient time learning these pinyin, as well as the very subtle differences with their correlated Chinese characters.

Pinyin	Chinese character(s)	English
Bà ba	爸爸	Dad
Gē ge	哥哥	Older brother
Gū gu	姑姑	Aunt (father's side)
Xiè xie	谢谢	Thank you
Mā ma	妈妈	Mom
Jiě jie	姐姐	Older sister
Shū shu	叔叔	Uncle (father's younger brother)
Kàn kan	看看	Look
Yé ye	爷爷	Grandfather (paternal)
Dì di	弟弟	Younger brother

Tài tai	太太	Wife
Shuō shuo	说说	Say
Nǎi nai	奶奶	Grandmother (paternal)
Mèi mei	妹妹	Younger sister
Xīng xing	星星	Stars
Cháng chang	常常	Often
Nǐ men	你们	You guys
Zhuō zi	桌子	Table
Shé tou	舌头	Tongue
Qián tou	前头	In front
Wǒ men	我们	Us
Yǐ zi	椅子	Chair
Zhěn tou	枕头	Pillow
Hòu tou	后头	Behind

Tā men	他们	Them
Bēi zi	杯子	Cup
Shí tou	石头	Stone
Lǐ tou	里头	Inside
Rén men	人们	People
Bèi zi	被子	Blanket
Mù tou	木头	Wood log
Wài tou	外头	Outside

Time

Being able to tell the time in Mandarin is vital. Not only might there be instances when clock faces show only the Chinese characters when telling time, but in terms of conversation, it is one of the most commonly asked questions to date. Whether you plan on reading time numerically or switching over to Chinese characters, it is important to spend some time on this section. Let's start with some context specific dialogues.

Context Specific Dialogues

Dialogue 1: Asking what the time is.

Person A: What is the time now?

                       现在几点?

                       Xiàn zài jǐ diǎn?

Person B: It is ten past ten.

现在十点十分。

Xiàn zài shí diǎn shí fēn.

Person A: When shall we have our lunch?

我们几点吃午餐?

Wǒ men jǐ diǎn chī wǔ cān?

Person B: At 12 o'clock.

十二点。

Shí èr diǎn.

Dialogue 2: Asking when someone will be returning.

Person A: When is father coming home?

父亲什么时候回家?

Fù qīn shén me shí hòu huí jiā?

Person B: At five o'clock this afternoon.

下午五点。

Xià wǔ wǔ diǎn.

Person A: When are we going to see the movie?

我们什么时候去看点电影?

Wǒ men shén me shí hòu qù kàn diǎn diàn yǐng?

Person B:	At half past six.
	六点半。
	Liù diǎn bàn.

Dialogue 3: Asking when someone will be departing and returning to an area.

Person A:	I'll go to Beijing next Tuesday.
	我下星期二要去北京。
	Wǒ xià xīng qí èr yào qù Běijīng.
Person B:	How long will you stay in Beijing?
	你要在北京待多久?
	Nǐ yào zài běi jīng dài duō jiǔ?
Person A:	For four days.
	四天。
	Sì tiān.
Person B:	Can you come back before Friday?
	你能星期五前回来吗?
	Nǐ néng xīng qí wǔ qián huí lái ma?
Person A:	Yes, I can.
	我可以。

Wǒ kě yǐ.

Telling the Time

Many will look at their watches or living room clocks and successfully be able to tell the time in English. However, what if someone is visiting and they ask you what the time is? Do you shy back into your comfortzone and answer in English? No, you remain confident in your abilities because you've studied Mandarin to this point, and you try to say it in Mandarin, even if you end up making mistakes.

To help you on your journey in becoming confident in telling the time in Madarin, here is a breakdown of different times and how they are translated into pinyin and Chinese characters.

English	Pinyin	Chinese characters
One o'clock	Yī diǎn	一点
Two o'clock	Liǎng diǎn	**两**点
Three o'clock	Sān diǎn	三点
Four o'clock	Sì diǎn	四点
Five o'clock	Wǔ diǎn	五点
Six o'clock	Liù Diǎn	六点
Seven o'clock	Qī Diǎn	七点
Eight o'clock	Bā Diǎn	八点

Nine o'clock	Jiǔ Diǎn	九点
Ten o'clock	Shí Diǎn	十点
11 o'clock	Shí yī Diǎn	十一点
12 o'clock	Shí èr Diǎn	十二点
Quarter past	...Shí wǔ Fēn	. . .十五分
Half past	...Bàn/Sān shí Fēn	. . .半/三十分
Quarter to	...Sì shí wǔ Fēn	. . .四十五分
Morning	Zǎo shang	早上
Afternoon	Zhōng wǔ	中午
Evening	Wǎn shàng	晚上
Midnight	Bàn yè	半夜

Let's really absorb the above information by tackling a few examples. Write the English times below in both pinyin and its respective Chinese characters. Take some time to rewrite the pinyin and Chinese characters in the spaces provided.

- Quarter past ten

十点十五分

_____

Shí diǎn shí wǔ fēn

● Quarter to two

一点四十五分

Yī diǎn sì shí wǔ fēn

● Five o'clock in the afternoon

下午五点

Xià wǔ wǔ diǎn

● 2:45 AM

凌晨**两**点四十五分

Líng chén liǎng diǎn sì shí wǔ fēn

● Quarter to midnight

晚上十一点四十五分

Wǎn shàng shí yī diǎn sì shí wǔ fēn

● Half past four in the afternoon

下午四点半

Xià wǔ sì diǎn bàn

- Quarter past seven

七点十五分

Qī diǎn shí wǔ fēn

- 5:00 AM

早上五点

Zǎo shang wǔ diǎn

- 11:30 AM

早上十一点半

Zǎo shang shí yī diǎn bàn

- Nine o'clock in the evening

晚上九点

Wǎn shàng jiǔ diǎn

Practice Dialogues

Focusing on the information that was just learned and combining it with the context specific dialogues, try your hand at the following practice dialogues. This specific set focuses on applying what you have learned and integrating it with common sentence structure, which you should have absorbed by this point. The practice examples that we would like you to complete are as follows:

Dialogue 1:

Xiàn zài jǐdiǎn?

现在几点?

What is the time?

Answer:

_____
_____
_____
_____
_____
_____

Dialogue 2:

Tā men jǐdiǎn chī fàn?

他们几点吃饭?

What time do they eat?

Answer:

_____
_____
_____
_____

Dialogue 3:

Bà ba shén me shí hou huí jiā?

爸爸什么时候回家?

What time does dad get home?

Answer:

_____

_____

_____

_____

Dialogue 4:

Tā men shén me shí hou qù kàn diàn yǐng?

他们什么时候去看电影?

What time will they go watch a movie?

Answer:

_____

_____

_____

_____

Dialogue 5:

Tā qù nǎr? Shén me shí hou néng huí jiā?

他去**哪**? 什么时候能回家?

Where did he go? What time will he be able to go home?

Answer:

_____

_____

_____

_____

_____

_____

Weather

At some point, you may have started to completely immerse yourself in your journey to learn Mandarin. This may even include watching Chinese news. This is a fantastic method for testing your level of conversational Mandarin. Furthermore, you want to ensure that you are able to understand a bit of what is being said. If you plan on visiting or living in a native Mandarin-speaking country, you will need to learn the basics in terms of understanding the weather. Naturally, being able to read weather forecasts will enable you to plan your days ahead, especially if you commute to in-person Mandarin classes. Let's start off with a few dialogues to get the ball rolling.

Context Specific Dialogues

Dialogue 1: Asking how the weather is in Beijing.

Person A: How was the weather in Beijing yesterday?

                    昨天北京的天气怎么样?

                    Zuó tiān běi jīng de tiān qì zěn me yàng?

Person B:	It was too hot.
	太热了。
	Tài rè le.

Person A: What about tomorrow? What will the weather be like tomorrow?

那明天呢？明天天气怎么样？

Nà míng tiān ne? Míng tiān tiān qì zěn me yàng?

Person B:	It will be fine. Neither hot nor cold.
	还好。不热也不冷。
	Hái hǎo. Bù rè yě bù lěng.

Dialogue 2: Asking about the current day's weather.

Person A:	Will it rain today?
	今天会下雨吗？
	Jīn tiān huì xià yǔ ma?

Person B:	No, it will not rain.
	不，不会下雨。
	Bù, bù huì xià yǔ.

| Person A: | Will Miss Wang come today? |
| | 王小姐今天回来吗？ |

Wáng xiǎo jiě jīn tiān huí lái ma?

Person B:　　　　　　　　No, she will not. It is too cold.

不，她不会。太冷了。

Bù, tā bù huì. Tài lěng le.

Non-Context Specific Dialogue

Dialogue 3: Relaying to another person how the weather is making you feel.

Person A:　　　　　　　　How are you?

你好吗?

Nǐ hǎo ma?

Person B: Not very well. It is too hot, and I have no appetite.

不太好。太热了而且我也没胃口。

Bù tài hǎo. Tài rè le ér qiě wǒ yě méi wèi kǒu.

Person A: You should eat more fruit and drink more water.

你应该要多吃水果多喝水。

Nǐ yīng gāi yào duō chī shuǐguǒ duō hē shuǐ.

Person B:　　　　　　　　Thank you, Doctor. I will do this.

谢谢医生。我会这么做。

Xiè xiè yī shēng. Wǒ huì zhè me zuò.

The Different Types of Weather

It is important that the different weather conditions are well understood, especially so that you can communicate effectively with other Mandarin-speaking individuals. Due to the very specific climate that Asian countries experience, it is important to familiarize yourself with those conditions that are not common in your country, as that will be what you experience if you plan to visit or emigrate to a native Mandarin-speaking country. A few examples of different weather conditions are as follows:

English	Pinyin	Chinese characters
Sun	Tài yáng	太阳
Rain	Xià Yǔ	下雨
Hail	Xià Bīng báo	下冰雹
Thunder	Dǎ léi	打雷
Lightning	Shǎn diàn	闪电
Cloudy	Yīn chén	阴沉
Haze	Yīn mái	阴霾
Mist	Wù	雾

| Windy | Yǒu Fēng | 有风 |

Practice Dialogues

Using the above, answer the following dialogues as you have previously. This is the last chapter that is loaded with information. Therefore, please ensure that you thoroughly revise all of the information up until this point. The reason for this is that the following chapters will include purely reading and writing exercises. With that being said, here are the practice dialogues based on the 'weather' portion of this chapter:

Dialogue 1:

Zuó tiān Bě ijīng de tiān qì zěn me yàng?

昨天北京的天气怎么样?

How was the weather in Beijing yesterday?

Answer:

_____

_____

_____

_____

_____

_____

Dialogue 2:

Míng tiān tiān qì zěn me yàng?

明天天气怎么样?

How will the weather be tomorrow?

Answer:

_____

_____

_____

_____

_____

_____

Dialogue 3:

Jīn tiān huí xià yǔ ma?

今天**会**下雨吗?

Will it rain today?

Answer:

_____

_____

_____

_____

_____

Dialogue 4:

Wáng Xiǎo jiě huí lái ma?

王小姐回**来**吗?

Will Miss Wang come back today?

Answer:

_____

_____

_____

_____

Dialogue 5:

Tā de shē ntǐ zěn me yàng?

她的身体怎么样?

How is her body?

Answer:

_____

_____

_____

_____

_____

Chapter 4:

Reading and Writing

Well done! You have made it this far, and we are super proud of you for it. At this point, you should have a solid foundation of knowledge to successfully hold a conversation in Mandarin. It does not matter how basic the conversation is as you are further than where you initially started. However, although speech is important, it is not the sole use of Mandarin. You will be reading books in Mandarin, as well as trying your best to correlate the pinyin to its respective Chinese characters and even to English. This is why we have prepared a few short stories for you to read. These short stories will be supplied in English, pinyin, and Chinese characters. There will even be some fun questions that will help your comprehension skills.

As you read these short stories, identify the different pinyin, listen to your tones as you pronounce them, and circle any characters that you have not yet learned. You can link this character to its pinyin by following the syllables in the sentence, and then research it accordingly. What a way to continually boost your vocabulary, right? Get ready to build on your foundation, because this is where major strides will be made.

Reading Exercises

When we are practicing our reading, it is important that we are able to correlate the English words with their pinyin and corresponding Chinese characters. This is why the short stories that we have devised for you below contain content that has already been covered in either this workbook or in the first book. If you find yourself struggling, try moving a few characters backwards to one that you recognize. Match that character with the pinyin, then with the English translation in order to clarify the meaning of the passage and to add more knowledge to your repertoire. The questions that follow each short story will be based on the story, with answers being clear and to the point.

Short Story 1

Li Yang is a seven-year-old girl who felt very hungry one day. After she went to go and ask her mother what they were having for dinner, she was sent to go buy some bread. Li left the house and saw that the sun was shining even though the weather forecast had said it would rain. Li got to the store, bought some bread from the storekeeper, and on her way home, she saw her brother. Her brother's name is Xiang Yang, and he was also on his way home. They decided to walk together. When Li got home, she gave the bread to her mother, and that evening the family enjoyed sandwiches for dinner.

杨丽是**个**七岁小女孩，

有一天**她**感觉很饿。**她**去问**她**妈妈**晚**餐吃什**么**之后被派去买些
面包。丽离**开**家时外头太**阳**很耀眼，

即使**气**象报告有说**会**下雨。丽到了商店后，　跟店主买了些面包，
回家路上**碰**见了**她**哥哥。**她**哥哥叫扬翔，

也在回家路上。**她们决**定一起走回家。丽回家时把面包交给了
她妈妈然后**当晚晚**餐时家人享受了三明治。

Yáng Lì shì gè qī suì xiǎo nǚ hái, yǒu yī tiān tā gǎn jué hěn è. Tā qù wèn tā mā mā wǎn cān chī shén me zhī hòu bèi pài qù mǎi xiē miàn bāo. Lì lí kāi jiā shí wài tou tài yáng hěn yào yǎn, jí shǐ qì xiàng bào gào yǒu shuō huì xià yǔ. Lì dào le shāng diàn hòu, gēn diàn zhǔ mǎi le xiē miàn bāo, huí jiā lù shàng pèng jiàn le tā gē gē. Tā gē gē jiào Yáng Xiáng, yě zài huí jiā lù shàng. Tā men jué dìng yī qǐ zǒu huí jiā. Lì huí

jiā shí bǎ miàn bāo jiāo gěi le tā mā mā rán hòu dàng wǎn wǎn cān shí
jiā rén xiǎng shòu le sān míng zhì.

Questions:

Who is Li Yang's brother?/ 杨丽的哥哥是谁?/ Yáng Lì dí gē gē shì
shéi?

_____

_____

_____

_____

What did Li Yang's family eat for dinner?/ 杨丽的家人晚餐吃什么?/
Yáng Lì de jiā rén wǎn cān chī shén me?

_____

_____

_____

_____

What weather did Li Yang encounter as she went to the shop?/ 杨丽
去商店时是什么天气?/ Yáng Lì qù shāng diàn shí shì shén me tiān
qì?

_____

_____

_____

_____

Short Story 2

Chenguang Liu is a 14-year-old boy who wanted to become a doctor when he grew up. His mother and father supported his decision and made sure that he was studying hard. He sat at his desk one night looking at the stars and moon in the sky. Although it was raining, he could see the stars all gathered together. At one moment, he saw a shooting star. Chenguang was so happy that he saw it and immediately made a wish. He wished that one day he would fulfill his dream of becoming a doctor. As time went on, Chenguang studied very hard. Four years later, he wrote his college entrance exams and got a seat in a top college in China. He was making his dreams a reality.

刘晨光是一个十四岁的男孩，

他长大想要成为一名**医**生。他爸爸妈妈支持他的**决**定还确保他用功读书。有一天**晚**上他坐在他的书**桌**时仰望着夜空的星星**与**月亮。虽然在下雨，

他还是看的到星星聚集。突然他看到了一颗流星。晨光看见了很**开**兴还立刻许愿。他希望有一天能**梦**想成**真**成为一名**医**生。

随着时间流动，

晨光依然的用功读书。四年后他写了高考还得到中国顶尖大学的一个位子。他正在实现他的梦想。

Liú Chén Guāng shì yī gè shí sì suì de nán hái, tā zhǎng dà xiǎng yào chéng wéi yī míng yī shēng. Tā bà ba mā mā zhī chí tā de jué dìng hái què bǎo tā yòng gōng dús hū. Yǒu yī tiān wǎn shàng tā zuò zài tā de shū zhuō shí yǎng wàng zhe yè kōng de xīng xīng yǔ yuè liàng. Suī rán zài xià yǔ, tā hái shì kàn de dào xīng xīng jù jí. Tú rán tā kàn dào le yī kē liú xīng. Chén Guāng kàn jiàn le hěn kāi xìng hái lì kè xǔyuàn. Tā xī wàng yǒu yī tiān néng mèng xiǎng chéng zhēn chéng wéi yī míng yī shēng. Suí zhe shí jiān liú dòng, Chén Guāng yī rán de yòng gōng dú shū. Sì nián hòu tā xi ěle gāo kǎo hái dé dào Zhōng Guó dǐng jiān dà xué de yī gè wèi zi. Tā zhèng zài shí xiàn tā de mèng xiǎng.

Questions:

How old is Chenguang Liu?/ 刘晨光几岁?/ Liú Chén Guāng jǐ suì?

_____

_____

_____

_____

How many years was it until Chenguang could take the college entrance exams?/ 晨光几年后才能高考?/ Chén Guāng jǐ nián hòu cái néng gāo kǎo?

_____

_____

_____

_____

What did Chenguang dream of becoming?/ 晨光有梦想成真吗?/ Chén Guāng yǒu mèng xiǎng chéng zhēn ma?

_____

_____

_____

_____

Short Story 3

Dong Hai Zhang was told that on Tuesday he needed to bring his parents to school for show-and-tell. His teacher had given each student a chance to bring their parents in and let the class know what their occupation is. Dong Hai's mother is a dentist, and his father is an engineer. His parents had to be at school at two o'clock in the afternoon. Dong Hai felt rather nervous that his parents were coming to meet his classmates and speak about their jobs. As Dong Hai was sitting in class at a quarter to two in the afternoon, he knew that his parents would be there soon. His feeling of nervousness became excitement as his parents had never been to his school before. Once his parents had given their speech, Dong Hai was allowed to go home with them. This was one of the most special days that Dong Hai will remember forever.

张东海被告知说他星期二需要带他的爸爸妈妈到**学**校**来**。他老师给每**个学**生一个把爸爸妈妈带**来**和全班介绍他们的职业的机

会。东海的妈妈是一名牙医,

他爸爸是一名工程师。他爸爸妈妈需要下午**两**点到**学**校。他爸爸妈妈要在他同**学**们讲述他们的职业让东海感觉**蛮**紧张的。下午一点四十五分的时候东海在**教**室里坐着,

他以知他爸爸妈妈已经快到了。他的紧张感变成了激动应为他爸爸妈妈**从来没**有**来**过他**学**校。**当**他爸爸妈妈演讲完之后,

东海**被允许**跟他们回家。这是一**个**最特别的日子让东海**永生**难忘。

Zhāng Dōng Hǎi bèi gào zhī shuō tā xīng qí èr xū yào dài tā de bà ba mā mā dào xué xiào lái. Tā lǎo shī gěi měi gè xué shēng yī gè bǎ bà ba mā mā dài lái hé quán bān jiè shào tā men de zhí yè de jī huì. Dōng Hǎi de mā mā shì yī míng yá yī, tā bà ba shì yī míng gōng chéng shī. Tā bà ba mā mā xū yào xià wǔ liǎng diǎn dào xué xiào. Tā bà ba mā mā yào zài tā tóng xué men jiǎng shù tā men de zhí yè ràng Dōng Hǎi gǎn jué mán jǐn zhāng de. Xià wǔ yī diǎn sì shí wǔ fēn de shí hòu Dōng Hǎi zài jiào shì lǐ zuò zhe, tā yǐ zhī tā bà ba mā mā yǐ jīng kuài dào le. Tā de jǐn zhāng gǎn biàn chéng le jī dòng yīng wèi tā bà ba mā mā cóng lái méi yǒu lái guò tā xué xiào. Dāng tā bà ba mā mā yǎn jiǎng wán zhī hòu, Dōng Hǎi bèi yǔn xǔ gēn tā men huí jiā. Zhè shì yī gè zuì tè bié de rì zi ràng Dōng Hǎi yǒng shēng nán wàng.

Questions:

What occupations does Dong Hai's parents do?/ 东海的爸爸妈妈的职业是什么?/ Dōng Hǎi de bà ba mā mā de zhí yè shì shén me?

_____
_____
_____
_____

What time did Dong Hai's parents have to be at school?/ 东海的爸爸妈妈什么时间要到学校?/ Dōng Hǎi de bà ba mā mā shén me shí jiān yào dào xué xiào?

_____
_____
_____

_____

What day did Dong Hai's parents come to his school?/ 东海的爸爸妈妈星期几要到他的学校?/Dōng Hǎi de bà ba mā mā xīng qí jǐ yào dào tā de xué xiào?

_____
_____
_____

_____

Writing Exercises

By this point, you should feel rather comfortable with reading segments of pinyin and Chinese characters and being able to relate them to their English counterparts. This skill will not be perfected overnight and will require a large amount of time and effort. However, in this subsection, we are going to focus on writing. In this section, sentences in both English and Chinese characters will be provided. Your job is to write the pinyin in the space below each sentence. If you see a Chinese character that you do not know in pinyin, do a quick online search in order to add this extra knowledge to your repertoire.

1. When I visited Australia, I was shocked to see kangaroos roaming freely in the wild.

当我去澳大利亚时，看到袋鼠自由漫游时然我感到惊讶。

_____

_____

_____

_____

2. I struggle to fall asleep at night. The main reason for this is that I am always hearing mosquitos.

我很难在晚上入眠。最大的理由是应为我都一直听到蚊子的声音。

_____

_____

_____

_____

3. When I grow up, I want to be a singer. However, my parents think that being a lawyer is a better job for me.

我长大时相**当**一个歌手。可是我父母觉得**当**律师是一个对我比较好的职业。

_____

_____

_____

_____

4. I really cannot concentrate when people speak to me when I have to study.

当我需要看书时**当**其他人跟我讲话时我无法专注。

_____

_____

_____

_____

5. Sometimes I find it rather difficult to understand what people say when they speak English.

有时候其他人讲英文时我发现很难理解。

_____

_____

_____

_____

6. I miss being a child and kicking the leaves when it was autumn.

我怀念幼年时在秋天**踢**落叶。

_____

_____

_____

_____

7. Everytime I ask someone what the best medicine is, they say it is laughter.

每次我问其他人那**个**药是最好的时候，　他们都**会**回是欢笑。

---

8. My parents taught me to always apologize when I have done something wrong.

我父母亲一直**叫**我**当**我做错事时要道歉。

---

9. Before I go to bed, I make sure to take my medicine and brush my teeth.

我上床时都**会**检擦我有吃完药刷完牙。

---

10. When I eat spicy food, my eyes tend to tear up, and people start to think that I am crying.

当我吃辣时，我眼睛都**会**流**泪**这让他人以为我在哭。

---

11. My mom gave me a necklace that was given to her by her mother. I always make sure that it is hanging around my neck.

我妈妈给我一**条她**妈妈给**她**的项链。我无时无刻都把**它**戴在脖子上。

12. Yesterday, I was laying on my bed with my hand on my chest. I was so shocked when I could feel my own heart beating.

昨**晚躺**在床上时**双**手放在胸前。我感到很**惊**讶我能感觉到我的心跳。

13. When I was five years old, my dad taught me how to plant a tree.

我五岁时我爸爸**教**我如何**种**树。

14. It was only when I pricked myself that I realized roses have thorns.

当我扎到我自己时我才发掘玫瑰有刺。

15. I was taught to always make sure to water my plants, especially when the soil is dry.

我被**教**说要确保给我的植物浇水，　特别是土壤干燥时。

Idioms

In order to really understand the roots of Chinese culture, one needs to be able to comprehend some of the most common idioms that are taught to youngsters and adults. Idioms allow us to think differently about our everyday lives, which is what the Chinese culture aims to promote. Typically, those of Chinese descent aim to be better individuals with each passing day. This is how China has become the thriving country that it is.

With the idioms below, the English translations are based off of a rough translation of the direct meaning implied by the story. Therefore, do not look too deeply into the English grammar, but instead, try to focus on the core meaning that is being portrayed.

Idiom 1

Title: A Promise Is Worth More Than a Thousand Gold Pieces/诺千金/Yī Nuò Qiān Jīn

During the Qing Dynasty, there was a man named Ji Bu. He was very straightforward, chivalrous, and loved to help people. If he was to promise something, no matter how hard the task was, he would think of a plan to complete the task, which received praises from everyone. At the time, there was a man named Cao Qiu Seng. He was a man who liked to suck up to power and wealth which made Ji Bu despise him. When Cao Qiu Seng heard that Ji Bu received a high official position, he immediately went to visit Ji Bu. When Cao Qiu Seng entered the hall, he immediately started bowing to Ji Bu and wanting to chat with him. Ji Bu did not want to take note of his presence, so Cao Qiu Seng started to flatter Ji Bu by saying, "Have you heard about a famous local saying that goes by 'receiving a thousand gold pieces is worth less than a promise from Ji Bu'? All your virtuous actions were made known by me, who has helped you spread the news everywhere." Ji Bu was immediately happy and treated him warmly. Afterward, Cao Qiu Seng carried on spreading the news, and Ji Bu's name became more famous.

Receiving a thousand gold pieces is worth less than a promise from Ji Bu. No matter how we treat people or do something, we need to keep our promises. This way we will be welcomed by others and respected.

秦朝时, 有一个叫季布的人, 性情耿直, **侠**义好助。只要是他答的 事情, 无论**怎样难办**, 他都设法办到, 受到大家的赞扬。**当时**, 有一个人叫曹邱生喜欢攀权附贵,

季布很看不起他。他听说季布做了大官,

就去见季布。曹邱生一进厅堂, 立即对着季布就是打躬, 作揖, 要**与**季布**叙旧**。季布不肯搭理他,

曹邱生就吹捧说: "**您**听说过楚地的民谚'得**黄**金千**两**,

不如得季布一诺'吗?

您的美德广为流传。那是因为我在替**你**宣传。"

季布听了顿时高兴起**来**，热情款待他。后**来**,曹邱生又继续替季布到处宣扬，季布的名**声**也就越**来**越大了。

得**黄**金千**两**，不如得季布一诺。我们做人做事要信守诺言的,才**会**受到大家的欢迎尊敬.

Qín cháo shí, yǒu yī gè jiào Jì Bù de rén. Xìng qíng gěng zhí, xiá yì hào zhù. Zhǐ yào shi tā dá de shì qíng, wú lùn zěn yàng nán bàn, tā dōu shè fǎ bàn dào, shòu dào dà jiā de zàn yáng. Dāng shí, yǒu yī gè rén jiào Cáo Qiū Shēng xǐ huān pān quán fù guì, jì bù hěn kàn bù qǐ tā. Tā tīng shuō jì bù zuò le dà guān, jiù qù jiàn jì bù. Cáo Qiū Shēng yī jìn tīng táng, lì jí duì zhe Jì Bù jiù shì dǎ gōng, zuò yī, yào yǔ Jì Bù xù jiù. Jì Bù bù kěn dā li tā, Cáo Qiū Shēng jiù chuī pěng shuō: "Nín tīng shuō guò dàng dì de mín yàn' dé huáng jīn qiān liǎng, bù rú dé Jì Bù yī nuò ma? Nín dì měi dé guǎng wèi liú chuán. Nà shì yīn wèi wǒ zài tì nǐ xuān yáng." Jì Bù tīng le dùn shí gāo xīng qǐ lái, rè qíng kuǎn dài tā. Hòu lái, Cáo Qiū Shēng yòu jì xù tì jì bù dào chù xuān yáng, Jì Bù de míng shēng yě jiù yuè lái yuè dàle.

Dé huáng jīn qiān liǎng, bù rú dé jì bù yī nuò. Wǒmen zuò rén zuò shì yào xìnshǒu nuòyán de, cái huì shòu dào dà jiā de huān yíng zūn jìng.

Idiom 2

Title: Both Lose and Are Severely Injured/ 两败俱伤/ Liǎng Bài Jù Shāng

During the Warring State Dynasty, there was an individual called Chun Yu. He was very clever and could always find many different solutions to different problems. He also had a good sense of humor.

When he heard the King of Qi state, Qi Xuan, was preparing to wage war and attack the Wei state, he immediately went to meet the king, hoping to convince him not to declare war against the Wei state. He told king Qi Xuan a story about the best hound and the most well-known and cunning rabbit. One day, when the hound was chasing the rabbit with the hope of catching him and eating him, the rabbit was running in the front with all of his might as his life depended on it. The hound was also found to be chasing behind the rabbit with all his might. The hound chased the rabbit for a long time. In the end, both of them ran out of so much energy they couldn't even move, after which both of them died of exhaustion at the bottom of the mountain. A farmer coincidently came across both the dead hound and cunning rabbit, and without needing to exert much energy, managed to carry them both home to skin and eat them.

King Qi Xuan asked Chun Yu, "I don't understand your meaning of telling me this story and what it has to do with me preparing to wage war against the Wei state." Chun Yu responded, "My king, if you were to go and wage war against the Wei state now, it is impossible to win the war in a short amount of time. In the end, both states will cause the civilians to suffer and become poverty stricken, the economy and treasury will collapse and deplete, and both sides will lose and become severely injured. And not only will the civilian's lives become unbearable, the military force will also receive a massive blow. If other states were to declare war against us now, we will have no power to defend ourselves, thus giving the other states a chance to conquer both the Qi state and Wei state." After listening to what Chun Yu said, King

Qi Xuan felt there was truth behind his words, so he immediately stopped all plans to wage war against the Wei state.

If two people, whose strengths and abilities are similar, start fighting against each other, not only will they not be able to decide a winner, but both sides will also become injured.

战国的时候，有一个名叫淳于的人，他很聪明，遇见事情时总是能想出很多好办法，讲话也很幽默。

当他知道齐宣王正在准备去攻打魏国时，就去见齐宣王，想要劝说他不要去攻打魏国。他给齐宣王说了一个关于最棒的猎犬和最有名的狡兔故事。有一天，猎犬追着狡兔，想要把他捉来吃了，狡兔在前面拼命地逃，猎犬在后头拼命地追。追了很久，结果他们两个都跑得没有力气不能动弹，

倒在山脚下死去了。这个时候刚好有个农夫路过，毫不费力就把他们两个一起带回家了吃掉。

齐宣王听完就问："我听不明白你说的这个故事和我现在去攻打魏国有什么关系？淳于回答大王现在去攻打魏国，在短期内是不可能打赢的，到头来双方都会弄得百姓贫穷，钱财尽失，两败俱伤，不仅老百姓生活艰苦，兵力也会大大受到损伤，如果到时其他国趁机攻打我们，不就是让他们有一并吞掉齐国和魏国的机会了吗。"
齐宣王听了淳于的话觉得很有道理，就停止了攻打魏国的计划。

如果两人实力相同互相打起来，不仅无法拼个胜负，还会造成双方受损。

Zhàn guó de shí hòu, yǒu yī gè míng jiào Chún Yú de rén, tā hěn cōng míng, yù jiàn shì qíng shí zǒng shì néng xiǎng chū hěn duō hǎo bàn fǎ, jiǎng huà yě hěn yōu mò.

Dāng tā zhī dào Qí Xuān Wáng zhèng zài zhǔn bèi qù gōng dǎ wèi guós hí, jiù qù jiàn Qí Xuān Wáng, xiǎng yào quàn shuō tā bù yào qù gōng dǎ Wèi Guó. Tā gěi qí xuān wáng shuō le yī gè guān yú zuì bàng de liè quǎn hé zuì yǒu míng de jiǎo tù gù shì. Yǒu yīt iān, liè quǎn zhuī zhe jiǎo tù, xiǎng yào bǎ tā zhuō lái chī le, jiǎo tù zài qián miàn pīn mìng de táo, lièquǎn zài hòu tou pīn mìng de zhuī. Zhuī le hěn jiǔ, jié guǒ tā men liǎng gè dōu pǎo dé méi yǒu lì qì bù néng dòng tán, dào zài shān jiǎo xià sǐ qù le. Zhèg e shí hòu gāng hǎo yǒu gè nóng fū lù guò, háo bù fèi lì jiù bǎ tā men liǎng gè yī qǐ dài huí jiā le chī diào.

Qí xuān wáng tīng wán jiù wèn: "Wǒ tīng bù míng bái nǐ shuō de zhè ge gù shì hé wǒ xià nzài qù gōng dǎ wèi guó yǒu shé me guān xì?" Chún yú huí dá: "Dà wáng xiàn zài qù gōng dǎ wèi guó, zài duǎn qí nèi shì bù kě néng dǎ yíng de, dào tóu lái shuāng fāng dū huì nòng dé bǎi xìng pín qióng, qián cái jìn shī, liǎng bài jù shāng, bù jǐn lǎo bǎi xìng shēng huó jiān kǔ, bīng lì yě huì dà dà shòu dào sǔn shāng, rú guǒ dào shí qí tā guó chèn jī gōng dǎ wǒ men, bù jiù shì ràng tā men yǒu yī bìng tūn diào Qí Guó hé wèi guó de jī huì le ma." Qí xuān wáng tīng le chún yú de huà jué dé hěn yǒu dào lǐ, jiù tíng zhǐ le gōng dǎ wèi guó de jì huà.

Rú guǒ liǎng rén shí lì xiāng tóng hù xiāng dǎ qǐ lái, bù jǐn wú fǎ pīn gè shèng fù, hái huì zào chéng shuāng fāng shòu sǔn.

Idiom 3

Title: Fifty Steps Laughing at a Hundred Steps/ 五十步笑百步/
Wǔshí Bù Xiào Bǎi Bù

During the Warring State Dynasty, the king of Liang State, Liang Hui, asked Mencius (a wise scholar in Chinese history) why his state could not increase the population count. He said, "I have put so much thought and energy into ruling the country, and I love and protect the civilians, yet I do not see any increase in the population numbers. What is the reason behind this?" Mencius replied with an example. "During warring times, while on the battleground, it is inevitable that there will be bloodshed. If some soldiers see that their side is at a disadvantage and losing position, it is inevitable that they will drop their weapons and shields to escape the battlefield. Now, if a soldier who has escaped with fifty steps sees another soldier who has escaped a hundred steps, yet he still laughs at the hundred step soldier and chides him for being a coward, is this correct?" King Liang Hui replied, "No, they are both the same." Mencius further said, "You say you love and care for your civilians and care for their hardships, yet at the same time, you love declaring war with the other states, causing many civilians to suffer and die in war. This is the same as if a soldier who has escaped with fifty steps laughs at another soldier who has escaped a hundred steps. Both of their actions are the same. Escaping is escaping." King Liang Hui thought about this in silence, and then finally decided to end the war.

During battle, when a soldier who has escaped fifty steps laughs at another soldier who has escaped a hundred steps, it is the same as you laughing at someone who has the same faults and shortcomings as you do. The only difference is the severity. You laugh at them without even noticing and being cognizant of your own faults and shortcomings. It is the same as 'the pot calling the kettle black'.

战国时期，

梁惠王向孟子请教为什么人口不增长的原因："我费心尽力治国，又爱护百姓，却不见百姓增多，这是什么原因？"，孟子做个比喻说："再战争的时候，战场上相遇，免不了要进行一场厮杀。如果有些士兵见状况不佳难免会弃甲逃离。如果一个跑五十步的士兵笑跑了一百步士兵，骂他是贪生怕死，这样对不对？"梁惠王回答："不对，两人都一样"孟子就说："你说你爱护百姓，关心百姓的艰苦，但同时你又喜欢和其他国战争，导致不少百姓死于战争。就像刚刚比喻的战争中逃了五十步的士兵嘲笑逃了一百步的士兵，逃跑的本质是一样的。"梁惠王默默思考，最后决定要停止打仗。

作战时，逃了五十步的士兵笑逃了百步的士兵，着比喻自己跟别人有同样的缺点错误，只是严重性请一些，却毫无自知之明的去嘲笑别人。

Zhàn Guó shí qí, Liáng Huì Wáng xiàng Mèng Zǐ qǐng jiào wèi shé me rén kǒu bù zēng zhǎng de yuán yīn: "Wǒ fèi xīn jìn lì zhì guó, yòu ài hù bǎi xìng, què bù jiàn bǎi xìng zēng duō, zhè shì shén me yuán yīn ne?", Mèng Zǐ zuò gè bǐyù shuō: "Zài zhàn zhēng de shí hòu, zhàn chǎng shàng xiàng yù, miǎn bu le yào jìn xíng yī chǎng sī shā. Rú guǒ yǒu xiē shì bīng jiàn zhuàng kuàng bù jiā nán miǎn huì qì jiǎ táo lí. Rú guǒ yī gè pǎo wǔshí bù dí shì bīng xiào pǎo le yī bǎi bù shì bīng, mà tā shì tān shēng pà sǐ, zhè yàng duì bù duì?" Liáng Huì Wáng huí dá: "Bù duì, liǎng rén dōu yī yàng" Mèng Zǐ jiù shuō: "Nǐ shuō nǐ ài hù bǎi xìng, guān xīn bǎi xìng de jiān kǔ, dàn tóng shí nǐ yòu xǐ huān hé qí tā guó zhàn zhēng, dǎo zhì bù shǎo bǎi xìng sǐ yú zhàn zhēng. Jiù xiàng gāng gāng bǐyù de zhàn zhēng zhōng táo le wǔshí bù dí shì bīng cháo xiào táo le yī bǎi bù dí shì bīng, táo pǎo de běn zhí shì yī yàng de." Liáng Huì Wáng mò mò sī kǎo, zuì hòu jué dìng yào tíng zhǐ dǎzhàng.

Zuò zhàn shí, táo le wǔshí bù dí shì bīng xiào táo liǎo bǎi bù dí shì bīng, zhe bǐyù zì jǐ gēn bié rén yǒu tóng yàng de quē diǎn cuò wù, zhǐ shì yán chóng xìng qǐng yī xiē, què háo wú zì zhī zhī míng de qù cháo xiào bié rén.

Idiom 4

Title: Hearing a Hundred Times Is Not as Good as Seeing It Once/ 百闻不如一见/ Bǎi Wén Bù Rú Yī Jiàn

During the Western Han Dynasty under the rule of Emperor Xuan, the Qiang people invaded the borders of Han. They attacked the border towns and cities, conquering land, burning down everything, killing, robbing, and stealing. Emperor Xuan gathered all his subordinates to discuss and come up with a counterattack. He asked who was willing to lead the army to fight back the enemy.

A 76-year-old old general, Zhao Cong Guo, had previously been at the borders and had interactions with the Qiang people for many years. He courageously volunteered himself to take up this important task. When Emperor Xuan asked how many soldiers and horses he needed for this task, Zhao Cong Guo said, "My king, don't listen to what other people say a hundred times. It's better to go see for yourself once. It is difficult to plan and calculate how to use the soldiers properly from afar. I am willing to go there myself to see the conditions, then come up with a battle plan for the attack and defence, draw up the battle map, and then report to the emperor."

After the approval of Emperor Xuan, Zhao Cong Guo led a squadron of soldiers and set off. After the squadron crossed the Yellow River, they ran into a small army of the Qiang people. Zhao Cong Guo ordered his squadron to charge and attack. Very soon, they managed to capture a lot of captives. The morale of the soldiers was very high, and they were preparing to chase after the escaped enemies. However, Zhao Cong Guo stopped them and said, "My squadron has already traveled far to reach this place, we must not carry on the pursuit. If we were to fall into an ambush from the enemy, we will suffer greatly!"

When his subordinates heard this, they were in awe of the old general's experiences. Zhao Cong Guo observed the terrain and also found out about the plans and situations of the Qiang people's army from the mouths of the captives, understanding the enemy's strengths and deployments. He then came up with a plan to defend the borders, stabilize the border areas, and disrupt and dismantle the Qiang people's armies and plans, which he proposed to Emperor Xuan.

Very soon, the Imperial Court sent out armies to stabilize the disruptions caused by the Qiang people and secured the northwestern borders.

That is why it is always better to see and experience something for yourself than to hear it from other people multiple times.

西汉宣帝的时候，羌人侵入边界。攻城夺地，烧杀抢掠。宣帝召集群臣计议，询问谁愿领兵前去抗敌。

七十六岁的老将军赵充国，曾在边界和羌人打过几十年的交道。他自告奋勇，担当这一个重任。宣帝问他要派多少兵马，赵充国说："陛下听别人讲一百次，不如亲眼一见。在遥远的地方算计好用兵是很难的。我愿意亲自到那里去看看，然后确定攻守计划，画好作战地图，再向陛下上奏。"

经过宣帝的同意，赵充国带领一队人马出发。队伍渡过黄河，遇到羌人的小股军队。赵充国下令冲击，一下子捉到不少俘虏。兵士们准备乘胜追击，赵充国阻拦说："我军长途跋涉到此，不可远追。如果遭到敌兵伏击，就要吃大亏！"

部下听了，都很佩服老将的见识。赵充国观察了地形，又从俘虏口中得知敌人内部的情况，了解到敌军的兵力部署，然后制定出屯兵把守，整治边境，分化瓦解羌人的策略，上奏宣帝。

不久，朝廷就派兵平定了羌人的侵扰，安定了西北边疆。所以说凡事自己看过经历过会比从旁人打听多次还有效。

Xī Hàn Xuān Dì de shí hòu, Qiāng rén qīn rù biān jiè. Gōng chéng duó de, shāo shā qiǎng lüè. Xuān Dì zhào jí qún chén jì yì, xún wèn shéi yuàn lǐng bīng qián qù kàng dí.

Qī shí liù suì de lǎo jiàng jūn Zhào Chōng Guó, céng zài biān jiè hé Qiāng rén dǎguò jǐ shí nián de jiāo dào. Tā zì gào fèn yǒng, dān dāng zhè yī gè zhòng rèn. Xuān Dì wèn tā yào pài duō shǎo bīng mǎ, Zhào Chōng Guó shuō: "Bì xià tīng bié rén jiǎng yī bǎi cì, bù rú qīn yǎn yī jiàn. Zài yáo yuǎn dì dì fāng suàn jì hǎo yòng bīng shì hěn nán de. Wǒ yuàn yì qīn zì dào nà lǐ qù kàn kàn, rán hòu què dìng gōng shǒu jì huà, huà hǎo zuò zhàn dì tú, zài xiàng bì xià shàng zòu."

Jīng guò Xuān Dì de tóng yì, Zhào Chōng Guó dài lǐng yī duì rén mǎ chū fā. Duì wǔ dù guò huáng hé, yù dào Qiāng rén de xiǎo gǔ jūn duì. Zhào Chōng Guó xià lìng chōng jí, yī xià zi zhuō dào bù shǎo fúlǔ. Bīng shì men zhǔn bèi chéng shèng zhuī jí, Zhào Chōng Guó zǔ lán shuō: "Wǒ jūn cháng tú bá shè dào cǐ, bù kě yuǎn zhuī. Rú guǒ zāo dào dí bīng fú jí, jiù yào chī dà kuī!"

Bù xià tīng le, dōu hěn pèi fú lǎo jiàng de jiàn shì. Zhào Chōng Guó guān chá le dì xíng, yòu cóng fú lǔ kǒu zhōng dé zhī dí rén nèi bù de qíng kuàng, liǎo jiě dào dí jūn de bīng lì bù shǔ, rán hòu zhì dìng chū tún bīng bǎ shǒu, zhěng zhì biān jìng, fēn huà wǎjiě Qiāng rén de cè lüè, shàng zòu Xuān Dì.

Bù jiǔ, cháo tíng jiù pài bīng píng dìng le Qiāng rén de qīn rǎo, ān dìng le xī běi bian jiāng.

Suǒ yǐ shuō fán shì zìjǐ kàn guò jīng lì guò huì bǐ cóng páng rén dǎtīng duō cì hái yǒu xiào.

Idiom 5

Title: A Word Seals the Deal/ 一言为定/ Yī yán wéi dìng

During the Warring State Dynasty, a man named Shang Yang from the Qing state wanted to change and reform the way the state was governed. When the new laws and regulations were created and confirmed, Shang Yang wanted to establish the seriousness of the new laws and regulations. He placed a log at the southern gate of the capital city and announced, " Whoever is able to carry this log all the way to the northern gate of the capital city will be rewarded with ten gold pieces." Everyone thought this action was strange, so no one dared to move the log. Later, Shang Yang raised the reward to fifty gold pieces. There was a man who was skeptical of this but still went to carry the log. He carried the log from the southern gate all the way to the northern gate. He even received the reward of fifty gold pieces. It was then that the people of the state decided that whatever Shang Yang said they would do. Afterward, Shang Yang announced the new laws and regulations.

When someone says and promises something, he/she should not then change it. It is to say that humans must be held accountable for their words and must never regret making their own decisions. People should ensure that they do not go back on the promises that they have made.

战国时,

商秧想在秦国变法革新。当新的法令编制制定好了一后,

商鞅为了要树立新法的威信, 他在首都的南门立了根木头, 公布说: "谁能把这根木头搬到北门, 就赏给他十**两**金子。"大家都感到奇怪,

所以**没**人敢动这跟木头。商秧又把赏金提高到五十**两**。那时有一个人**将**信将疑地去搬了, 他把那块木头**从**南门搬到北门, 结果**真**的得到了五十**两**赏金。人们这才相信商秧说话是算**数**的。商鞅**随**后就颁布了新法令。

一句话说定了, 就不再更改**它**。比喻一个人说话要算**数**, **决**对不能翻悔。

Zhàn Guó shí, Shāng Yāng xiǎng zài Qín Guó biàn fǎ gé xīn. Dāng xīn de fǎ lìng biān zhì zhì dìng hǎo le yī hòu, Shāng Yāng wèi le yào shù lì xīn fǎ de wēi xìn, tā zài shǒu dū de nán mén lì le gēn mù tou, gōng bù shuō: "Shéi néng bǎ zhè gēn mù tou bān dào běi mén, jiù shǎng gěi tā shí liǎng jīn zi. "Dà jiā dōu gǎn dào qí guài, suǒ yǐ méi rén gǎn dòng zhè gēn mù tou. Shāng Yāng yòu bǎ shǎng jīn tí gāo dào wǔ shí liǎng. Nà shí yǒu yī gè rén jiāng xìn jiāng yí de qù bān le, tā bǎ nà kuài mù tou cóng nán mén bān dào běi mén, jié guǒ zhēn de dé dào le wǔ shí liǎng shǎng jīn. Rén men zhè cái xiàng xìn Shāng Yāng shuō huà shì suàn shǔ de. Shāng Yāng suí hòu jiù bān bù le xīn fǎ lìng.

Yī jù huà shuō dìng le, jiù bù zài gēng gǎi tā. Bǐyù yī gè rén shuō huà yào suàn shù, jué duì bù néng fān huǐ.

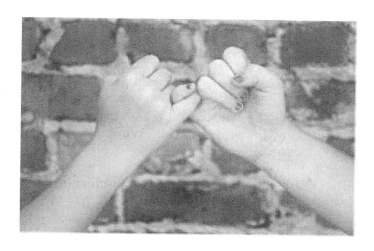

Idiom 6

Title: The Frog in the Well/ 井底之蛙/ Jǐng Dǐ Zhī Wā

There was once a frog that lived in a deserted well. One day, the frog was resting on top of the well fence, and suddenly, he saw a massive turtle coming out of the sea. He shouted to the turtle, "Hey, brother turtle, please come over. Hurry and come over!"

The frog boastfully said to the turtle, "Look, look how happy I am living here! When I am happy, I can hop around the well fence for a while; when I get tired, I can return into the well and sleep inside a hole in the brick wall of the well or quietly float around the water whilst leaving my head and mouth above water. Or take a walk in the soft mud, which is very comfortable. Furthermore, I am the owner of this well. I am free and unbound within this well. I bet you have never seen such a wide and spacious dwelling? Why don't you come to the well often to browse around?"

After listening to the frog about the well, the turtle actually wanted to take a look inside. When the turtle stuck his head out into the well to see, all he saw was a shallow well with a few puddles of water covered with moss. There was also a very pungent smell that wafted against the turtle. The turtle hurriedly took two steps back and decided to tell the frog about the sea. "Have you ever seen the sea? Th e sea is vast, even wider than a thousand miles; the sea is so deep, it's even deeper than thousands of feet. In the past, out of ten years, there were nine years of flooding, yet there was minimal change in the rise of the sea levels. Afterward, out of eight years, there were seven years of drought, yet there was no sign of the sea levels dropping. It is evident that the sea level is unaffected by drought or flood. Living in the sea is what true happiness is!"

After the frog heard about the sea, he was dumbfounded and at a loss for words.

有一只青蛙住在一口废井里。有一天，青蛙在井栏上休息，突然碰上了一只从海里来的大乌龟。它对着乌龟喊，"喂，乌龟兄，请过来，快过来！"

青蛙就对海龟夸口说："你看，我住在这里多快乐！有时高兴了，就在井栏边跳跃一阵；疲倦了，就回到井里，睡在砖洞边一回。或者只留出头和嘴巴，安安静静地把全身泡在水里；或者在软绵绵的泥浆里散一回步，也很舒适。而且，我是这个井里的主人，在这井里自由自在，你大概从来也没有见过这样宽敞的住所吧？你为什么不常到井里来游赏呢！"

那乌龟听了青蛙的话，倒真想进去看看。乌龟探出它的头往井里看看，只见浅浅的井底积了一摊长满绿苔的泥水，还闻到一股扑鼻的臭味。它连忙后退了两步，把大海的情形告诉青蛙说："你看过海吗？海的广大，哪止千里；海的深度，

哪只千来丈。古时候，十年有九年大水，并不涨了多少；后来，八年里有七年大旱，

海里的水, 海里的水,

也不见得浅了多少。可见大海是不受旱涝影响的。住在那样的 大海里，才是真的快乐呢！"

井蛙听了海龟的一番话， 吃惊地呆在那里， 再没有话可说了。

Yǒu yī zhǐ qīng wā zhù zài yī kǒu fèi jǐng lǐ. Yǒu yī tiān, qīng wā zài jǐng lán shàng xiū xí, tú rán pèng shàng le yī zhǐ cóng hǎi lǐ lái de dà wū guī. Tā duì zhe wū guī hǎn," wèi, wū guī xiōng, qǐng guò lái, kuài guò lái!"

Qīng wā jiù duì hǎi guī kuā kǒu shuō: "Nǐ kàn, wǒ zhù zài zhè lǐ duō kuài lè! Yǒu shí gāo xìng le, jiù zài jǐng lán biān tiào yuè yī zhèn; pí juàn le, jiù huí dào jǐng lǐ, shuì zài zhuān dòng biān yī huí. Huò zhě zhǐ liú chū tóu hé zuǐbā, ān ān jìng jìng de bǎ quán shēn pào zài shuǐ lǐ; huò zhě zài ruǎn mián mián de ní jiāng lǐ sàn yī huí bù, yě hěn shū shì. Ér qiě, wǒ shì zhè ge jǐng lǐ de zhǔ rén, zài zhè jǐng lǐ zì yóu zì zài, nǐ dà gài cóng lái yě méi yǒu jiàn guò zhè yàng kuān chǎng de zhù suǒ ba? Nǐ wèi shé me bù cháng dào jǐng lǐ lái yóu shǎng ne!"

Nà wū guī tīng le qīng wā de huà, dào zhēn xiǎng jìn qù kàn kàn. Wū guī tàn chū tā de tóu wǎng jǐng lǐ kàn kàn, zhǐ jiàn qiǎn qiǎn de jǐng dǐ jī le yī tān zhǎng mǎn lǜ tái de ní shuǐ, hái wén dào yī gǔ pū bí de chòu wèi. Tā lián máng hòu tuì le liǎng bù, bǎ dà hǎi de qíng xíng gào sù qīngwā shuō: "Nǐ kàn guò hǎi ma? Hǎi de guǎng dà, nǎ zhǐ qiān lǐ; hǎi de shēn dù, nǎ zhǐ qiān lái zhàng. Gǔ shí hòu, shí nián yǒu jiǔ nián dà shuǐ, hǎi lǐ de shuǐ, bìng bù zhǎng le duō shǎo; hòu lái, bā nián li yǒu qī nián dà hàn, hǎi lǐ de shuǐ, yě bù jiàn dé qiǎn le duō shǎo. Kě jiàn dà hǎi shì bù shòu hàn lào yǐng xiǎng de. Zhù zài nà yàng de dà hǎi lǐ, cái shì zhēn de kuài lè ne! "

Jǐng wā tīng le hǎi guī de yī fān huà, chī jīng de dāi zài nà lǐ, zài méi yǒu huà kě shuō le.

Conclusion

You have heard that studying Mandarin is not easy. However, you have now bypassed one of the hardest parts of learning the language: the beginning. Many who want to learn Mandarin believe that there are too many rules that need to be followed. We have proven that this is not the case. In the first book, you found all the rules condensed in a systematic manner. This should have not only improved your understanding of the subject matter, but hopefully, it also started to make you feel more comfortable with learning Mandarin.

Fast-track a few hours of reading and study later, you would have begun working through this workbook—one that has been filled with a penultimate amount of new words and phrases coupled with everything that you need in order to have a conversation in Mandarin. You have surpassed the most difficult part of learning Mandarin, and that is the creation of your foundation. Some get scared when they see tones on words, and others assume that writing Chinese characters is too difficult to learn. However, you have overcome all of these perceived notions about learning Mandarin and are now ready to take your journey even further!

Having completed this workbook, you are prepared to tackle the HSK 1 examinations that were spoken about in the previous book. This feeling of achievement and success once passing this test will motivate you to start looking at content to pass the HSK 2 examinations. At this point, you should have a rather in-depth view of how Mandarin sentences are constructed, whether it be in pinyin or in Chinese characters. Now, the focus shifts from learning basic words to understanding more advanced sentence and phrase construction.

With the abundance of different Chinese characters present, your learning and studying will never be completed. Understanding Mandarin requires you to be a life-long learner. Having gotten this far, it is safe to say that you definitely know what is required of you in order to succeed as an individual who is studying Mandarin.

References

Bin, Y. (n.d.). *Chinese for HSK 1*. Coursera. Retrieved January 3, 2021, from https://www.coursera.org/learn/hsk-1

Borgers, M. (n.d.) . *HSK1 exam preparation*. QuizzerWiz. Retrieved January 4, 2021, from https://www.quizzerwiz.com/hsk1-exam-preparation/

/how-to-learn-languages/9-steps-to-overcome-the-fear-of-speaking-a-foreign-language

Global Exam. (2016, September 7). *HSK Level 1 Online Training: skills required to pass the exam*. GlobalExam Blog. https://global-exam.com/blog/en/hsk-1-online-training/

Huizhongmcmillen, A. (n.d.). *Easy as ABC: 8 Foolproof Tips for Learning Chinese Faster*. Retrieved January 4, 2021, from https://www.fluentu.com/blog/chinese/2016/01/18/tips-for-learning-chinese/

Pinyin Guide. (n.d.). *Pinyin Guide | Pronunciation, FAQs and more*. Pinyin Guide. Retrieved January 5, 2021, from https://www.pinyin-guide.com/

Wang, K. (2018, August 13). *How to study for Chinese HSK 1 exam - Quora*. Www.Quora.com. https://www.quora.com/How-do-I-study-for-Chinese-HSK-1-exam

Yi, L. (2013). *Introduction to Chinese Characters | Year of China*. Www.Brown.Edu. https://www.brown.edu/about/administration/international-affairs/year-of-china/language-and-cultural-resources/introduction-chinese-characters/introduction-chinese-characters#:~:text=Oracle%20Bone%20Inscriptions%20refers%20to

All images were obtained using Pixabay.

Made in the USA
Las Vegas, NV
03 October 2023

78527915R00154